THE CHALLENGE OF ISLAM TO CHRISTIANS

The Challenge of Islam to Christians

David Pawson

HODDER &
STOUGHTON

First published in Great Britain in 2003

10 9 8

British Library Cataloguing in Publication Data
A record for this book is available from the British Library

ISBN-13: 9780340861899

Typeset in Times by Avon DataSet Ltd,
Bidford-on-Avon, Warwickshire

Printed in the UK by CPI Group (UK) Ltd, Croydon, CR0 4YY

The paper and board used in this paperback are natural recyclable
products made from wood grown in sustainable forests.
The manufacturing processes conform to the environmental
regulations of the country of origin.

Hodder & Stoughton
A Division of Hodder Headline Ltd
338 Euston Road
London NW1 3BH
www.madaboutbooks.com

Contents

Foreword by Michael Green

This is a fascinating book which will gain a wide readership and stir up a variety of emotions. I am very pleased to have the privilege of commending it to the study of thoughtful Christians who care about their faith, because I think it is likely to prove one of the most significant religious books published this year.

What makes it so special?

In the first place, the origin of the book makes it special. Islam and its challenge to Christianity is not a topic that David Pawson had spent much time on previously. And yet, as he relates in the Prologue, he was being prepared for it over many years. The sudden conviction that he should tackle the subject came to him in the midst of a talk by the Islamic specialist Canon Patrick Sookhdeo. David is well known for the fact that at times a prophetic gift comes to him and drives him in a certain direction, and that is what happened on this occasion. Consequently, the book is written with an unusual and deep sense of compulsion.

Secondly, this book is special because to tackle such a subject is perilous. It would so easily render the author liable to the charge of narrow-mindedness, lack of charity or even racism. The book is certainly not politically correct, and makes no attempt to be. In an age when it is commonly thought that all religions lead to God, and that it is improper to criticise any of the world's religions, David Pawson has some highly critical things to say about both Christianity and Islam. He is not out to attack either of these great faiths, but he is pointing out weaknesses which need to be recognised, and incompatibilities which have to be faced.

Thirdly, this book is special because of its theme. Pawson believes, with good reason, that Islam is the greatest external challenge to Christianity. It is growing much faster than the Christian faith, and is spreading widely over the globe. Many of its leaders have expressed the goal of world supremacy, to bring all people to the obedience of Allah. Moreover he shows that Christianity, at least in the West, is in poor shape and utterly unable to withstand the youthful enthusiasm and aggression with which Islam prosecutes its cause. He foresees the day, not indefinitely removed, when an effete Western Christianity will not be able to stand up to the vigorous advance of Islam, which is already the second largest religion in the world. The massive numbers of immigrants from Islamic lands coming into Britain, and the feeble grasp on Christianity of many of the churches combine to persuade him that England is very likely to succumb to the passionate convictions of the Muslims, who already nearly equal the size of the established church in these islands. This suggestion is no scare tactic, but a carefully documented examination of the comparative confidence of the adherents of the two faiths in spreading their beliefs. Muslims have already targeted twelve major cities in Britain. England might soon become a Muslim country. If that seems wildly improbable, read on!

David Pawson does not claim to be an expert on Islam, but he is well read and has spent time in Islamic lands. I am no expet on the subject, but his information seems to me to be well founded and accurate; it presents the crescent advancing and the cross declining in this once Christian country. I am very impressed at the restrained and gentle way in which he handles these contentious issues. There will be those who violently oppose his thesis, of course, but they will not, I think, be able to cavil at the gracious way he makes his points.

The book falls into two parts: the Islamic resurgence and the Christian response. The first part of the book is required reading for anyone who thinks this thesis is scaremongering; the second is no less requisite for any who feel that Christianity in this land is doomed. Once again the prophetic chord is struck. David believes that reality, relationship and righteousness are three key words borne in upon him by God's Spirit for Christians to take to heart. He mused on the words for a long time, and Chapters 8–10 are the result. They could stand on their own as an introduction to authentic Christianity.

Chapter 11 wrestles with the issue of whether reconciliation is possible between Christians and Muslims. David Pawson makes it abundantly clear that the Christian God and the Muslim Allah are very different, but in the spirit of his master, he is concerned not so much with confrontation as with clear sighted reconciliation.

The final chapter is the most controversial. He believes that in the last analysis Islam is false and will not be able to stand at the return of Christ, and he dares to expound and apply the rather obscure New Testament teaching about the Antichrist and the great Tribulation. While Muslims believe that Jesus will return to show himself a devout Muslim and to lead the human race back to Islam, Christians believe Jesus will return to save Israel 'as a whole'; to defeat the Antichrist; bind and banish the devil from the earth; and reign over this world for 1000 years before the final judgement which will usher in a new universe for renewed people. There will be no place for other religions then: at the name of Jesus every knee will bow.

Not all Christians will agree with Pawson's reflections on the end. Nor will all welcome his conclusion about Islam. But few can argue with his three final questions – will we survive, will we suffer, and will we swell? (That is to say, will we have the enthusiasm and passion to spread the gospel, yes, even to Muslims?) He concludes that if we cannot do it now, we shall not do it then. But no, that is not quite his last word. He invites readers to go back and read those three central chapters – on our knees.

Some years ago I believed that the future lay either with an aggressive Communism, a resurgent Islam or a renewed Christianity. Now only two of those options remain. With great courage an internationally known teacher, David Pawson, has stuck his neck out and invited us to face the alternatives – and act in the light of our conviction. It is a bold book, and it is immensely significant to us all because, since 9/11, we simply cannot hide our heads in the sand about the relationship of the two greatest faiths in the world. We have to make up our minds.

Canon Dr Michael Green
Advisor on Evangelism to the
Archbishops of Canterbury and York

Foreword by Patrick Sookhdeo

David Pawson has sounded a wake-up call to the Church in the UK. The British Church increasingly faces not just a loss of members but also a lack of theological certainty and conviction. The ravages of secularisation have taken their toll on her and pluralism has marginalised her, creating a vacuum which Islam is now fast filling.

From analysing the nature of contemporary British society David Pawson moves on expertly to describe the growing influence of Islam in Britain. Over the last hundred years, Islam has grown at a phenomenal rate. From a religion which seemed to have no future it is now vibrant, confident and assured. In the British context, its growth and increase in the post-war period have been considerable, and it is now established with structures, institutions and networks. It is a part of the British landscape and is increasingly moving towards a position of dominance.

This book is not primarily about Islam but rather about the dangers facing Christians and the Church in the UK. It is a most timely and crucially important work. Not everyone will agree with all that it contains, but it throws light on a subject which British Christians cannot afford to ignore any longer.

David Pawson has shown great courage in seeking to face the Church with unpalatable truths.

Rev Dr Patrick Sookhdeo
Director, Institute for the Study of Islam
and Christianity in London

Prologue

I looked in the mirror and a stranger stared back at me. One side of his face hung down, twisting his mouth at an odd angle.

I knew immediately I was the victim of a stroke. But the family doctor was not so sure, suspecting Bell's palsy, since only the face was seriously affected. It was a matter of weeks before I could get a proper diagnosis from a consultant neurologist, who confirmed a stroke. However, tests revealed that blood pressure, artery flow, sugar and cholesterol levels were all well within normal limits. An MRI brain scan revealed clear damage to the cranial nerves affecting my throat, tongue and lips and that is still apparent, months later.

The physical setback gained significance from preceding and following events.

A few weeks before, I had been speaking at a Pentecost camp for over thirty thousand Christians on a polder in the Zuider Zee in Holland, where I had picked up a virulent throat infection. Twenty-four hours later, I had flown to America to address a national convention and speak at seminars up to six hours per day. A three-plane journey brought me home exhausted. But I had rested for a week and was much relaxed when stricken out of the blue. Was this 'nature' or even the Lord telling me to be my age (I'm in my seventies) and ease up on my itinerating ministry?

But an engagement a few weeks after seemed to throw a very different light on my condition. I had committed myself to making an all-day recording, audio and video, on the subject of this book: 'The Challenge of Islam to Christians'. A room at Waverley Abbey in Surrey had been booked, expensive equipment hired and an invited audience informed. Now it looked as if it could not be done.

Word about my problem spread rapidly, even on the Internet. Hundreds prayed that I would have sufficient speech and stamina to record this vital message, many convinced that 'the enemy' was trying to prevent the message from being given and released. In the event, I was able to speak for five and a half hours, though towards the end I was having to stand on one leg, my left side in the grip of cramp (men in the front row told me afterwards they were poised to catch me). Anyway it was 'in the can'.

Response has been phenomenal. Tapes have been demanded by thousands here and overseas. The message has attracted attention in the media: press, radio and television. Now my publishers, Hodder & Stoughton, have requested this book, which enables me to expand and explain my burden.

The most surprising aspect is that until January 2002, I had no interest in, much less intention of, addressing this subject; others having far greater knowledge and experience of Islam than I. Yet in hindsight, I can see that I was being prepared for it over five decades, the second half of the twentieth century.

In the 1950s, I had been a chaplain in the Royal Air Force and was posted to its base in Aden. My 'parish' stretched along the south coast of Arabia through Riyan, Salalah and Masirah, up the Persian Gulf through Sharjah to Bahrein and included visits to Yemen, Somaliland, Ethiopia and Kenya. I was in the heartland of Islam. My wife, first child and I lived in an Arab town inside the crater of an extinct volcano, reached through a tunnel in the rim. Awakened each morning by the muezzin call to prayer, we got used to seeing men pray at street corners throughout the day. As 'OD' (other denominations than RC and C of E) chaplain I was responsible for Muslim airmen as well, my first 'duty' to ensure their diet was free from pork fat. I learned we had to be very careful during Ramadan since tempers were more volatile with the daily fasting and nightly feasting. I remember the shock of encountering the rough amputation of a thief's hand in the market place; the expression on his face, while his stump was cauterised in pitch, haunted my dreams. From a third-floor balcony I saw a bunch of excited men dragging a naked woman by her hair in the dust; I wanted to intervene but friends told me it was the law, the penalty for adultery being death by stoning, the same in Muslim law as in the Mosaic. Above all, I discovered that the death penalty also applied to any who converted from Islam to Christianity, baptism being the focal point of such an act of 'treason' (which led me to re-examine and later refuse the christening of babies). This first experience of living abroad was something of a culture shock and I cannot say I was unhappy when flown home as a 'casevac' (casualty evacuation).

In the 1960s, I paid the first two of seventeen visits to Israel. One was purely nostalgic, to see the places mentioned in the Bible. The second, right after the famous 'Six Day War', drew my attention to the people now living in the places. Touring the Golan Heights with an Israeli major, picking our feet over live ammunition, I asked how they had taken these hills packed with Russian-made guns; by way of answer, he simply pointed to the sky. It was during that astonishing conflict that I reached two conclusions, which have been controlling convictions ever since. The first was that God has not finished with his chosen people (I had never really noticed that the New Testament already said this in Romans 11). The second was that the troubles in the Middle East are religious as well as political, spiritual as well as social, theological as well as geographical, involving two gods as well as two peoples. Subsequent history has deepened both beliefs.

In the 1970s, a new note crept into my preaching. I found myself saying that Islam was a far greater threat and challenge to Christianity than Communism, though we were still in the Cold War. When the Shah of Persia celebrated the two-thousand five-hundredth anniversary of his country and gave himself a new title: 'King of Kings and Lord of Lords', I announced his fall, which took place shortly after. I had not anticipated his replacement by the Ayatollah Khomeini, whose establishment of the Muslim (Shariah) law turned a pro-Western regime into an anti-Western one (Iran). It was an ominous precedent.

In the 1980s, I was due to take part in an Easter Saturday march, culminating with a public preaching in a car park. Around midday my wife and I were driving along the Mile End Road in East London towards the magnificent new mosque when its doors burst open and hundreds of men, many in their prime, poured into the street, holding up the traffic for some time. Later, we drove on to our destination, and walked down a high street the next day with a few hundred Christians. But women outnumbered men and the men were either young or older, few in their prime. On the way home I asked my wife, if she were a gambler, which religion she'd put her money on; her instant response was: 'Obviously, Islam'. The stark contrast stayed in my mind.

In the 1990s, Ahmed Deedat, a Muslim propagandist based in South Africa, challenged any British Christian to debate the rival merits of Islam and Christianity in the Royal Albert Hall in Kensington. Clive Calver, then director of the Evangelical Alliance, urged me to enter the ring. But I was very reluctant, having heard about my opponent's persuasive charm and sharp intellect, and suggested other far more able candidates. None would take it up so it came back to me. However, when the event was advertised my name had been replaced by that of an Arab evangelist from America. Though relieved, I would like to have been informed of the switch and feared he was not well known enough in the UK to draw much Christian support and that the Muslim speaker would mock our failure to produce a British defender of the faith. All my fears were realised and the largely Muslim audience revelled in the clear victory of their champion, so much so that the Alliance disassociated itself from a repeat performance in Birmingham. In retrospect, I believe I was preserved from a premature confrontation, since I was far from ready for such a challenge. Nor was the time ripe.

The new century contained three significant events linking me again with Islam.

The first was the horrific disaster of '9/11', the collapse of the twin towers of the World Trade Center in New York, after being hit by aeroplanes hi-jacked by suicidal pilots. Like many, I saw it actually happen on television. The biggest shock was not the fragility of the structures, nor the appalling loss of life including rescuers, but that it was deliberately done in the name of religion, the name of the god of Islam,

Allah. Five days later I spoke to a group of churches in Southampton. While concentrating on the fundamental question of why God allows such suffering, I included some comments on the religious factor, which many found enlightening. The world now wanted to know more about this faith and whether such acts of terror were a true or distorted expression of it. Tapes of my talk went far and wide and led many to repentance as they took God more seriously (six adult children of one man all came to faith through it and the rejoicing father died a few months later).

The second was a visit to a nearby grammar school. A mullah had been invited to speak about Islam and the school was buzzing with interest in this unfamiliar religion. A concerned member of staff (not the Head of Religious Studies, a declared atheist!) begged me to come and restore interest in Christian things – if he could persuade the headmaster to give me fifteen minutes in an assembly. He did and I faced 850 boys and thirty teachers. It had taken days to prepare such a short talk (longer ones take much less!), which would later become the basis for Chapter 9 in this volume. By all accounts it achieved its purpose, and interest in the novelty was replaced with a concern for the truth, for which I am truly grateful.

The third was a meeting I attended in Reading in January 2002, little dreaming that it would radically change my life, from a very gradual retirement to being right back in the public eye. The announced speaker was Dr Patrick Sookhdeo, who has graciously written a foreword for this book. I went along simply to get a little more insight and information concerning Islam, from an acknowledged expert on the subject.

In the middle of his talk, both unexpected and unrelated to its contents, I was suddenly overwhelmed with what could be described as a premonition that Islam will take over this country. I recall sitting there stunned and even shaking. We were not just listening to an interesting lecture about a religion and culture, which others believed and practised. We were hearing about our own future!

The shock of this awareness remained with me long afterwards. I did not share it with anyone for weeks while I tried to grapple with its implications. And where had this thought come from – my own subconscious or a supernatural prompting, from above or below, divine or demonic? The way in which I came to believe it was a 'prophetic' revelation from God I will reserve for a later chapter (7).

Suffice it to say at this stage that an alarming number of Christian leaders with whom I eventually shared my concern encouraged and even urged me to make it public, adding that I was the right person to do this. I've never had so many volunteering to stick my neck out! Perhaps they knew I had less to lose, having no pulpit, no organisation, no charitable trust, no office, not even a secretary, only my reputation – and I threw that away years ago.

So that is how I set out on this venture and why I am now writing this book. Only the Lord knows what it could lead to, but my future is in his hands. And my book is in yours.

Speakers and writers are warned not to begin with a lot of negative statements, but I feel I must break with this convention and tell you what this book is *not*, to avoid disappointment, misunderstanding, controversy and unnecessary offence.

It is not intended to be a manual of information about Islam. Others have done a far better job of that (for an introduction, you can't do better than to read Dr Patrick Sookhdeo's *A Christian's Pocket Guide to Islam*). I am bound to include both facts and statements about this religion, but I must emphasise that these are not the results of primary research but have been culled from numerous publications by Christian and Muslim authors, whose accuracy I must depend upon and cannot guarantee. The conclusions drawn are my own.

It is not intended to be an attack on Muslims. I would be grieved if this material caused or was used to stir up fear and hatred of Islamic followers. These two emotions feed each other. Some Christians are already too intimidated and this can easily become an irrational and paralysing phobia, issuing in racist attitudes and actions. All Muslims are fellow human beings made in the image of God and for whom our Lord Jesus Christ laid down his own life. If divine love includes them, so must ours. And if we have been saved by grace, so can they be.

It is not intended to be a course of instruction on how to evangelise Muslims, in spite of the last paragraph. Others have far more wisdom and experience in this field than I, and helpful guidance may be found in any Christian bookshop. I would simply make two observations here. First, serving and saving must go together in this mission. Second, signs are needed as well as words and deeds, and healing is particularly effective in opening hearts.

Let me finish on a positive note. This book is intended for Christian readers, though if it falls into Muslim hands I dare to believe it will convey the gospel to them. But I have written out of a burden for the Church and the thrust of the whole book, particularly Part Two (Chapters 7–12), is a wake-up call to Christians to prepare themselves for what lies ahead. The title has been very carefully chosen and says it all.

Part One

The Islamic Resurgence

1

Its Spread

Islam is now a universal phenomenon.

It is the second largest religion in the world, claiming at least one fifth of the population, one and a half-billion. Christianity has one third.

It is the fastest-growing religion in the world, over four times the rate of Christian increase.

Its followers may be found on five continents and in 165 countries, forming the majority in forty-five Asian and African states, of which the largest are Pakistan, Bangladesh, Indonesia and Iran.

If present trends continue, half the global births will be in Muslim families by the year 2055. In some quarters, Islam has already been given an accolade of '*the* religion of the twenty-first century'.

The advent and advance of this faith, the latest of the great world religions, constitute an astonishing story, covering the last fourteen centuries. It all began with one forty-year-old man who, apparently, could neither read nor write.

Since our subject is its spread, we will trace the history geographically, beginning with its starting point: Arabia.

ARABIA

This huge peninsula is largely barren desert, with a monotone landscape of sand and sky. When our story begins it was sparsely inhabited by a number of travelling tribes, often fighting each other for survival in such a barren environment. But there were some settled centres of population, which focused on trade routes and the junctions where camel caravans exchanged goods. Among these, the major one was Mecca, in the centre.

The town was also a religious centre. Surprisingly for such simple surroundings, faith was much more complex, believing in many spirits ('jinn'; we call them 'genies') and many gods (we call this 'polytheism'). Mecca was a hub of religious practice, centred on a tall stone building, nearly a cube in shape (hence *Ka'aba* in Arabic), containing 360 idols to be worshipped (one for every day of the lunar calendar, twelve months of thirty days). The moon played a special role in desert life and was believed to be a male god, while the sun god was female and therefore inferior; they had three 'daughters', two of whose names were compounds of *allah*, the word for 'god'. Archaeologists have unearthed a number of stone altars with a crescent moon carved on them (a symbol now seen on the pinnacle of mosque domes). Pilgrims to the shrine would walk round the *Ka'aba* seven times and kiss a black stone embedded in its exterior wall, which may have been a meteorite. In all this, it is significant that 'gods' were associated with visible features in a desert existence, from stones to stars.

One group prospered from this mixture of trade and religion in Mecca, the Quraish tribe, into which Muhammad was born, around AD 570, shortly after his father (Abdullah, servant of *allah*) died. Losing his mother at six, he was brought up by a succession of relatives. He found work in the caravan trade, employed by a wealthy widow, Khadijah, whom he later married, though she was fifteen years older.

His travels brought him into contact with Jews and Christians, encountering a belief in one God (monotheism) which challenged the polytheism of his background. With a sensitive and retiring disposition, he would retreat to a mountain cave for meditation. It was here that he had the first physical and spiritual experience, at the age of forty, which with later such encounters, over three decades, led him to claim to be the 'prophet' of the one God 'Allah', the last and final messenger to reveal his will to the human race.

His bold opposition to polytheism, on which the popularity and prosperity of Mecca to a large degree depended, naturally led to tension with his own tribe, eventually forcing him to flee for his life to Medina. This flight (the Hijrah), in AD 622, marks the first year in the Muslim calendar, for in this refuge, his family and friends, his first followers, formed the first community believing in and living by his revelations. These covered marriage and divorce, forbade alcohol and usury and introduced the concept of 'jihad', holy war. They were engaged in many fights, notably with forces from Mecca. After some setbacks, Muhammad gathered superior forces and marched on Mecca, and the city surrendered to his rule. He showed some magnanimity towards defeated foes but destroyed all their idols. From here the ripples of holy conquest spread far and wide throughout the whole land, though 'the Prophet' returned to spend his remaining years in Medina, where he died and was buried, in AD 632, 11 AH, at the age of sixty-three.

By that time he had succeeded in uniting the whole of his country under the rule of Allah, with the by-product of unity between the hitherto warring tribes, who were now beginning to think of themselves as a nation. It was an astonishing achievement, virtually of one life and lifetime, or rather, just twenty years. It is hardly surprising if Muslims explain it as the work of one God through his greatest prophet.

Even more amazing is the expansion of this Arabic religion over the next century. The nation would become an empire so quickly.

THE MIDDLE EAST

The first thrust was to the north, encompassing what was then called 'Palestinia' and the city of Jerusalem. Though it is not named in the Quran, it became the third holiest city of Islam, after Mecca and Medina, because Muhammad had a vision (or dream) in which he rode a horse to heaven from this city. The Mosque of Omar ('Dome of the Rock') would soon be built there as a challenge to Jews (it was erected on the site of their temple) and Christians (on an inside wall was inscribed a Quranic verse, which said: 'Far be it from God to have a son').

Jerusalem fell in 634 and Damascus, capital of Syria, followed a year later. This northern advance was finally stopped near Constantinople by an army of the 'Christian' Byzantine Empire.

Today there are over 300 million Arab Muslims in the Middle East, over half under the age of fifteen.

AFRICA

Simultaneously with this northern push was a western move. Egypt was conquered within a decade of Palestine and Syria.

This was welcomed by the Christians there, who had become somewhat heretical in the eyes of their Byzantine rulers and thought they could now be independent.

By 710 the Muslims had swept right along the North African coast, which had been a stronghold of early Christianity, noted for such influential figures as Clement and Origen of Alexandria and Augustine, Bishop of Hippo, which is now in Tunisia. The churches were virtually swept into oblivion.

Arab traders (and slaves) sailed their dhows down the east coast of Africa, taking their religion with them to places like Zanzibar. Islam is today well established in South Africa, Durban being the base of Ahmed Deedat, one of their best-known apologists.

Islam has crossed the Sahara and is pressing down into nations on the west coast. Nigeria is typical. Its northern region, around Kano, is solidly Muslim. The middle region is controlled by Muslims, though Christians are in the majority. The south is still largely Christian.

There are today over 300 million Muslims in the continent of Africa.

ASIA

The success in Islamicising Asia may be measured by the number of nation states whose names end with the suffix '-stan'. There is a cluster of them in southern Russia and surrounding Persia, now Iran. Recent events have focused attention on Afghanistan, as the home of militant Muslim groups.

When British control of India came to an end after World War Two, it was partitioned between Hindu and Muslim governments, accompanied by much bloodshed and migration of refugees. This resulted in two Muslim nations in the north: Pakistan and Bangladesh. What is not often realised is that there are still 100 million Muslims in India itself.

From the Indian sub-continent Islam spread further east. Malaysia, another former British colony, is now a Muslim country, though other faiths are tolerated, provided they do not proselytise Muslims. Indonesia is even less tolerant, as recent attacks on Christians show.

Asia as a continent now has the greatest Muslim population, with nearly 800 million, all the more remarkable since it has involved the acceptance of Arabic language, culture and architecture into a very different indigenous tradition.

EUROPE

This continent became the heartland of Judeo-Christian culture, exporting this 'Western' civilisation to the rest of the world through a mixture of imperial colonisation and missionary enterprise.

There have been three kinds of Muslim incursion – military, mental and migratory.

The military invasion began within the first wave of Islamic expansion. Having conquered the North African coastline, Muslim forces crossed to Gibraltar in 711, conquered Spain and swept into France, coming within 70 miles of Paris. They were defeated in the battle of Poitiers in 732, the centenary of Muhammad's death. But Spain remained in their hands for some centuries, renamed al-Andalus (Andalusia), with Cordoba as its capital. Only in 1492, the year Christopher Columbus discovered America, did this occupation end.

The second invasion of Europe came from the east rather than the west. In 1071 the 'Christian' Byzantine army was defeated by the Seljuk Turks. The Emperor appealed to the Pope for help, which ultimately led to the infamous and disastrous Crusades, ostensibly to free the shrines of Holy Land pilgrimage from Muslim control.

The Ottoman Empire was established in 1281 and conquered the Byzantine capital in 1453. Constantinople was now Istanbul, its huge central church of St Sophia became the Grand Mosque, now a museum. The Balkans had been defeated at the Battle of Kosovo in 1389 (ironically, British soldiers recently found themselves defending Muslims against Serbian Christians!). Muslims pressed on to besiege Vienna but were finally repulsed in 1682. Ottoman control of the Middle East ended in 1918, in spite of German backing.

The mental influence of Islam on the whole of Europe is little known and hardly realised, though far surpassing the remnants of military invasions. Most have heard of the 'Enlightenment', that 'age of reason' which has dominated Western culture and civilisation ever since. Some have heard of its alternative name, the 'Renaissance', pointing to the rediscovery of the achievements of the ancient 'classical' world of Graeco-Roman philosophies, arts and sciences. Few are aware of the vital role played by Arab Muslims in this intellectual revolution.

From the tenth century AD, the Muslim world developed a remarkably sophisticated culture, even civilisation, focused on Baghdad (now the capital of Iraq). A philosopher, Farabi, who had been taught by Christians, was known as 'the second Aristotle'. Greek literature was ransacked for wisdom and translated into Arabic. In three particular fields – mathematics, medicine and architecture – the ancient classical world came alive again and was developed (the 'invention' of the zero is at the heart of computer technology today and, of course, we still use Arabic numerals). Anyone who visits Granada's Alhambra Palace in Spain or the Taj Mahal in India cannot fail to be impressed with their beauty and symmetry.

It was in the twelfth century that Jewish and Christian scholars in Spain, particularly Toledo, began to translate Greek works and Muslim commentaries on them from Arabic into Latin. The foundations were laid for a revolution in European life and thought.

Before leaving this theme, we must note three spiritual phases through which this intellectual endeavour passed. The Arabs took over much that was Greek but without their polytheism, without their many mythical gods and goddesses. For them, all intellectual pursuits were within the framework of the monotheism of Allah and were to be used for his glory. However, the Europeans took this heritage over without either the Greek or the Arab theological setting. For all practical purposes, the Enlightenment was atheist, rendering belief in gods or God irrelevant and superfluous even while still giving lip service to deism (the belief that God created the universe but is no longer in control of it).

But the contemporary incursion of Islam into Europe, particularly its northern nations, is neither aggressive nor academic. It is due to massive migration. In a sense it is the long-term effect of the imperial history of these same nations. Muslims pour back into the 'mother' countries from their former colonies, Algerians into France, Pakistanis into Britain.

The two main objectives of this mobility are prosperity and protection. Some seek the obvious economic advantages for themselves and their families. Probably the majority of legal immigrants are in this category. Others flee from the despotic regimes which seem to flourish in Islamic countries, perhaps inevitably under a religion that favours autocracy rather than democracy. The majority of illegal immigrants are probably in this category.

And they bring their religion with them. While some are 'assimilated' into the secular society into which they have come, the majority maintain their spiritual loyalty, both to preserve their identity by maintaining its roots and their moral standards when they discover the decadence that surrounds and disgusts them. This has led many to believe they have a unique contribution to make in saving the Western world from complete moral and social anarchy, giving them an unexpected sense of mission. And in this developing self-confidence they find some sympathy from their new neighbours.

As long ago as 1936, George Bernard Shaw, the Irish playwright who made his home in Hertfordshire north of London, wrote:

If any religion had the chance of ruling over England, nay Europe, within the next hundred years, it could be Islam. I have always held the religion of Muhammad in high estimation because of its wonderful vitality. It is the only religion which appears to me to possess that assimilating capacity to the changing phase of existence which can make itself appeal to every age. I have studied him – the wonderful man and in my opinion far from being an anti-Christ, he must be called the Saviour of Humanity. I believe that if a man like him were to assume the dictatorship of the modern world, he would succeed in solving its problems in a way that would bring it the much needed peace and happiness. I have prophesied about the faith of Muhammad that it would be acceptable to the Europe of tomorrow as it is beginning to be acceptable to the Europe of today.

(from *The Genuine Islam*, Vol. 1, No. 8, 1936, and accessible on the Internet)

A remarkable prophecy, with only thirty years left in which to be fulfilled!

In the next chapter we shall look at the particular case of the United Kingdom and its predisposition to welcome the presence of Islam. Prime Minister Blair is pressing for the inclusion of Turkey in the European Community, even though most of it lies in Asia. Founded as a secular republic after World War One, its population of about 80 million is almost entirely Muslim and in a recent election lurched to the religious right. It would be second in size to Germany, with which it was allied in both world wars.

THE AMERICAS

In South America, Muslims are still a relatively small minority. It is the least Islamicised continent (apart from Antarctica!).

North America reflects the European situation, partly due to its very open (until recently) policy towards immigration. There are now millions of Muslims, but one third of these belong to the black Muslim sect, which has its own theological version, and is unacceptable to orthodox Islam. Overall, Islam is the second largest and fastest-growing religion, as it is in most of the world, with mosques springing up like mushrooms in all major US cities. But then religious diversity has been more welcome there than anywhere else.

The spread of Islam has not been even or steady. Waves have advanced and receded, but each has been further up the beach. This new twenty-first century (on the Christian but not the Muslim calendar) is witnessing a forward surge, particularly in the Western world, hence the title of the first half of this book. It is marked by a new self-confidence among Muslims, which is not unrelated to two developments in the Islamic heartland of the Middle East.

One is the release of Arab nations from the colonial control of European powers such as Britain and France. Two world wars gave them political autonomy. This very objective motivated the exploits of 'Lawrence of Arabia'. They are now players on the world stage in their own right. This development also explains their increasing resentment of America's cultural invasion and military intervention, which have replaced the former European incursion into their territory. This anger is naturally focused on the support of a Western-style state of Israel in the area.

The other factor is the discovery of huge reserves of oil ('black gold') beneath their lands. Together with increasing dependency of the Western economy on this commodity, this has brought untold and unexpected wealth and influence in world markets.

The newly acquired political and financial power has boosted the self-assurance of Muslims worldwide. We close with remarks made at the opening of a mosque in Stockholm:

In the next fifty years we will capture the Western world for Islam. We have the men to do it; we have the money to do it; and, above all, we are already doing it.

2

Its Opportunity

In Britain today there is a huge spiritual vacuum, as there is throughout Europe. Human nature, as well as nature, abhors a vacuum. There is a god-shaped blank in the soul that cries out to be filled.

So a religion already surging ahead can be sucked into such a vacuum, the momentum of both movements reinforced by each other. This is the position of Islam in Britain. Its arrival has coincided with an unprecedented opportunity.

Christianity has been the traditional religion established by law and nominally part of life from national (coronation of monarchs, prayers in parliament) to individual (births, marriages, deaths) levels. But popular recognition of this is in sharp decline. One set of statistics revealed that the Established Church was losing 1,000 souls a week and the largest Free Church was closing two buildings a week. At most, only 10 per cent of the population attend worship services each Sunday. While there are some large churches with membership into four figures, these are in cities of millions and the ratio of insiders to outsiders is little better than elsewhere.

What has caused this disastrous decline (alas, in quality as well as quantity), amounting to a haemorrhage? The answer must reach back into the last few centuries, which have introduced a number of 'isms' into the fabric of British inner beliefs and outer behaviour.

I am allergic to most 'isms', which usually pose a threat, even in a Christian context (Anglicanism, Methodism, Lutheranism) – though I can accept evangelism and baptism!

What follows can be no more than a thumbnail sketch of the more general 'isms' that have invaded Britain. Some readers may find the survey superficial and simplistic but I believe that these are the threads that must be woven into any analysis of contemporary society.

We must begin inside the mind. There has been a radical change in the way we think. The roots go back 400 years. Then, the source of truth was what God had revealed to us through the Bible (Protestant northern Europe) and/or the Church (Catholic southern Europe). Then came the 'Enlightenment' with its claim that humans could discover the truth for themselves, without God's help. Three 'isms' took over, one after another.

RATIONALISM

Rationalism was the first in the field, putting its hope in human reason. The mind was the seat of learning and the method was scientific observation and experimentation. What was not able to be 'proved' in this way could not satisfy the intellectual demand and was dismissed with scepticism. Scientism (the proper name for believing that all truth can and must have this kind of 'proof') soon came into conflict with Scripture, focusing on the debate between creation and evolution.

Sometimes known as 'modernism', this rational or cerebral approach to life was cold. It appealed to the mind, but not the heart. It failed to take into account that people are as much if not more motivated by what they feel as what they think. Inevitably, a reaction set in.

ROMANTICISM

In romanticism the heart was the seat of learning. The truth of life was to be found through emotion rather than investigation. The emphasis would be on art rather than science, from painting to poetry. Reality had to be felt.

The search for meaningful experiences began. Inevitably this would lead to the use of artificial stimulants and addictions to them. The line between fact and fantasy would be increasingly blurred.

This subtle shift from the outward to the inward search for truth, from the experimental to the existential, was to have profound effects.

RELATIVISM

The switch from facts out there to feelings in here, from the objective to the subjective, from 'modern' to 'post-modern', inevitably led to changes in belief and behaviour and attitudes to both. Absolute convictions gave way to relative opinions.

This was due to the great variety of human beings, caused by heredity and environment. Each individual is bound to think and feel in a different way from others. When what's true for all gives way to what's true for each, absolute standards disappear.

In matters of belief, no-one can claim a monopoly of the truth. All religions may have some truth, but none has all. The most that can be said is that Christianity is true for Christians, Islam is true for Muslims, Hinduism for Hindus and, of course, agnosticism is true for the agnostic and atheism for the atheist. To profess an exclusive knowledge of God is deeply offensive, since this is an absolute claim.

In matters of behaviour, application of moral 'standards' to the community gave way to a discussion of 'ideals' and 'values' of the individual and how far these could be shared.

Absolutes have opposites. What is true defines what is false. What is right defines what is wrong. Relativism abolishes such distinctions. Black and white are replaced with shades of grey.

Let us now look at some of the social repercussions of all this.

PLURALISM

Most Western countries are now multicultural and multi-religious, especially in urban areas. Liberal immigration policies and post-war migration from former colonies have particularly changed Britain into a 'plural' society. This has often been welcomed for introducing greater freedom of taste and choice, from food, cars and clothes to music and enter-tainment, though it has not always been without tension and conflict.

Pluralism, however, goes further than this by saying that such a mixture of culture is not only good, but necessary to social maturity. Diversity is a virtue when freed from the vice of disunity. Since none has the whole understanding of anything, all are needed as equally valid and valued contributions to a rich wholeness of life. Tact and tolerance are high on the list of social virtues.

There is some truth in this as far as culture is concerned, but it can be a dangerous approach to religion.

SYNCRETISM

There is an increasing pressure on the religions of the world to 'get it together', both for the sake of peace among peoples and for protection of the environment. Since none are believed to have all the truth, mutual exclusion is inexcusable. Better to forget our differences, acknowledge each other's way to God as valid and fight with unity against all that militates against our health and happiness.

The media now talk about 'the faith community' without distinguishing between the faiths, while recognising Christianity and Islam as its two most significant components. Joint action against 'social evils' is already under way. Even the Evangelical Alliance, formed to protect and proclaim the Christian gospel inside the Church, is now advocating such 'co-belligerence' outside it, for some limited political objectives.

But the crunch comes with shared acts of worship, which are already taking place, with praise and prayer offered to 'the God of Abraham, Jesus and Muhammad'. Some 'Festivals of Faith' throw the net wider. The present Pope called representatives of all the world religions to pray for peace with him, in Assisi, the home of St Francis. To withdraw from such 'ecumenical' (the word originally meant 'worldwide' and is returning to that usage) activity is to be labelled a bigot.

However, all this has not halted the decline of traditional religion in this country and may even be hastening it, as its distinctive contribution becomes less clear. Right now, irreligion is the order of the day for the majority.

SECULARISM

Since no religion is thought to have a monopoly of truth, none has the right to a dominant role in the life of a nation. Indeed, all should be allowed but none should be officially adopted.

This amounts to the privatisation of religion and its removal from public life and affairs. It becomes a matter of individual choice and preference, to be practised privately or only communally with those whose tastes coincide. It therefore becomes a leisure activity, indulged in after work or at weekends. Persuasive proselytising is discouraged, since this is a public invasion of privacy.

An international poll concluded that Britain is the second most 'godless' (i.e. irreligious) country in the world, beaten only by Japan! The Roman Catholic cardinal of Westminster caused a stir when he observed, accurately I think, that Christianity here was 'close to being vanquished' (he meant from the public sphere as the recognised religion).

The public image of religion is one of increasing irrelevance and obsolescence. So what takes its place? To what do people devote themselves? What governs their ambitions and actions? We will look at three final '-isms'.

MATERIALISM

Scientism claims that the physical universe is all the reality there is. It is not surprising if the search for meaning and purpose in life concentrates on the material world – what can be seen, heard, touched, even smelled.

And it means focusing on the world and this life, since science has not been able to find any other beyond the present one. In the absence of any obvious purpose for existence beyond survival, there has been a widespread assumption that happiness is the only worthwhile objective, which takes various forms, depending on whether its source is thought to lie in people or things.

HEDONISM

The pursuit of whatever brings pleasure and the corresponding flight from whatever brings pain explains a great deal of contemporary society, from an increasingly exotic tourist industry to an obsession with sexual orgasm, however obtained. Resorting to artificial stimulants, drink and drugs, fosters the escape from reality into fantasy.

One ingredient is absolutely essential – health. Since ill-health invariably brings pain or discomfort, a society devoted to enjoyment will become very health-conscious, even while adopting habits likely to undermine it. The demand for efficient public health services, excessive interest in diet and exercise, the rise of alternative medicine and profits made by pharmacies and health shops are all symptoms.

Most hedonism seeks sensual pleasure but another form desires a different satisfaction.

CONSUMERISM

The myth that multiplying possessions brings peace of mind is astonishingly widespread in the light of the evidence. If there is one thing that is very clear it is that contentment cannot be bought.

Again, one ingredient is absolutely essential to this quest – money. A society believing happiness is found in things will be desperate to get more wealth, by fair means or foul. Gambling, from lotteries to sharp deals in trading shares or money exchange, will be seen as a quicker way of amassing a fortune than earning it by service.

There will soon be more people shopping than worshipping on Sunday morning, whether in fields at car boot sales or in the modern 'cathedrals' of shopping malls. The IKEA catalogue has a circulation four times greater than the Bible. Governments stand or fall on how they handle the economy. The 'market' is all-powerful.

This all-too-brief survey is no more than a glance at straws on the water indicating the general direction in which Britain is heading. All nine trends listed are anti-Christian in particular and anti-religious in general. Together they explain why Christianity is now as much a minority faith as the others, whose only value in the eyes of the majority is a possible influence for good on social behaviour or the reduction of crime and poverty.

But this is not the whole story. Spiritual needs are not satisfied. There is still a vacuum in the soul that cries out to be filled. The 'god-shaped blank' is still there. Something or someone has to occupy it. If it is not the 'one true God', it will be an idol of some kind.

Much worship, which includes both adulation and

emulation, is directed towards human beings, 'stars' of pop, films and sport. A recent portrait of Victoria and David Beckham (the singer and footballer 'Posh and Becks') pictures them as Hindu gods to be added to that pantheon. Royalty can be so regarded, surfacing at moments of tragedy (Princess Diana's funeral) and triumph (Queen Elizabeth's jubilee). But sooner or later, 'feet of clay' are exposed and adoration switches to others.

And there is a reaction to Western materialism, often into Eastern mysticism. The Beatles were among the pioneers. A post-modern generation embraces 'spirituality', though it can take quite bizarre forms, some harmless but many dangerous. For a few it has meant a return to Christian tradition but for most what is novel has great attraction: varying mixtures of New Age and old occultism. Ancient paganism is having something of a revival. In fact, anything goes, especially among the young.

However, there is another possibility; namely, one of the existing world religions, new to British culture, could step into the gap and become the dominating faith in the country. And of the potential candidates, Islam is far and away the best placed to do so, its presence and influence visibly increasing. It is now the second largest and fastest-growing religion here, as it is in the rest of the world. Again, a brief sketch must suffice.

During recent decades the number of Muslims in Britain has risen from a few thousand to well over two million. The Bishop of London said that by 2004 there will be more Muslims than Anglicans in the UK. Most of this growth has been by immigration, both legal and illegal. The former has been from ex-colonies of the British Empire like Pakistan; the latter, ironically, is mainly refugees from Muslim countries like Afghanistan. Because of our generous welfare services, Britain is the preferred refuge.

But there are other factors. The Muslim birth rate is higher than that of the typical British family (and Christian families are little different). An increasing number of British women marry Muslim men and adopt their faith and lifestyle. And conversions are happening by the thousand, 'more than convert from Islam to Christianity', it is claimed.

From one mosque, built near Woking in Surrey and visible from the railway line to London, there are now over 2,000, some new and magnificent structures, while others are converted from pubs, shops, cinemas and redundant churches (the mosque in my home town, Basingstoke, is the former 'Gospel Hall' of the Christian Brethren). The largest was built in Regent's Park by one of the biggest contractors in Britain, founded by a Christian family called Laing and recently sold off for the princely sum of one pound.

There are large Muslim enclaves in many of big British cities, especially in the industrial Midlands and North of England, but supremely so in London. These are not ghettos since there is no imposed isolation, but become so concentrated by mutual attraction that they virtually become semi-exclusive communities.

Education is being infiltrated. Teaching comparative religion in state schools opened the door. Islamic exhibitions are held in primary schools. Study centres are being opened in universities: Oxford (funded from Sharjah) and Exeter (funded from Oman and Dubai) were the first, followed by the University of Wales. Muslims are opening their own schools (State-funded) and training colleges.

Politics is feeling the impact, both locally and nationally. There are Muslims in the House of Lords, one Conservative and the rest Labour. There is also an eagerness to favour minorities, with legislation on race relations, most recently against stirring tensions by 'defamation of religion', a difficult crime to define and apply. Other tensions between Islamic and British law, over marriage and inheritance for example, have yet to be resolved. In addition, British Muslims have now formed their own Party (1989), Parliament (1991) and Council of Britain, bringing together 250 organisations (1997).

Petrodollar investments have long been a feature of the commercial scene, particularly in London, where up to a fifth of bank reserves are involved and withdrawal could provoke a crisis. Trade with Middle East countries, especially in armaments, is a vital element in the British export market. Leading hotels and shops in London are owned by Arabs. Added to all this is British dependence on oil from Islamic countries in the Middle East.

There are now more Islamic books published in English than in Arabic; more Muslim newspapers in London than anywhere else. Since 11 September 2001, interest in Islam has rocketed and many colleges have introduced study courses in it. There have been so many programmes on television that the press refers to Channel 4 as 'The Voice of Islam'.

Public figures have added their share of publicity. A colour photograph of the Queen entering a mosque without shoes appeared on the same front page of a newspaper as a report of my prediction of a takeover. The Duke of Edinburgh is involved with a trust whose task is to produce a definitive English translation of the Quran. Princess Diana's romance with Dodi could have led to the first Muslim marriage in the British Royal Family. Dodi's father's hopes were so frustrated that he – Muhammad Al Fayed, owner of Harrods, the London store formerly patronised by royalty – is convinced their deaths were the result of a conspiracy, not an accident.

Prince Charles is quite open about his sympathy with Islam

and has already suggested that when he is crowned he wishes his title to be changed from 'Defender of the Faith', which has Christian connotations, to 'Defender of Faith', that is, of all religions, though Islam is foremost in his mind. Objectors to this change need to be reminded that the present title was conferred by the Pope on King Henry VIII for writing a treatise against Luther and Protestantism! The King's quarrel with and split from Rome was over divorce, not doctrine.

The former Prime Minister, John Major, opened a multi-media centre for Islam. The present Prime Minister, Tony Blair, admitted he now reads the Quran every day, but later claimed it was purely for the purpose of being informed about Islam after the New York disaster. He and President Bush of the Unites States are at pains to assure the world that the Anglo-American 'war against terrorism' has nothing to do with Islam even if intervention targets Muslim lands, such as Afghanistan and Iraq. Are they naïve enough to think that acts of terrorism done in the name of Allah have no link with Islam or is it propaganda to avoid inflaming the Arab world, the vital source of oil? Tony Blair's plea for including Turkey in the European Community, though most of it is in Asia, may spring from the same motivation. It would be the first Muslim State in a Union whose other members all have a Christian tradition.

Muslim leaders in Britain have been quite frank about their hopes of taking the United Kingdom for Allah and bringing not only Muslims but all of us under his laws (Shariah). To quote one: 'That must be our goal or we have no business here and may Allah give us success.' But this will be evolutionary rather than revolutionary, using talk rather than terror, persuasion rather than power, 'By waging psychological warfare while exhibiting the Islamic way of life', to quote another.

The Muslim community already has an influence out of proportion to its size and receives more publicity in the media than any other religion like Hinduism or Buddhism. This is partly due to our desperate desire to be 'politically correct' towards minorities and do nothing to deserve the label 'racist'. Criticism of other cultures and religions is taboo.

With influence has come a degree of intimidation, especially since a death sentence (fatwah) was passed on Salman Rushdie for his novel *The Satanic Verses* (for an explanation of why this was so offensive, see Chapter 6). Even in this country of free speech, a threat from as far away as Iran still meant that he had to go into hiding. Over the Christmas season of 2002, the British Red Cross forbade decorations in their 432 charity shops, lest Muslim customers took offence. The ironic thing is that the suggestion did not come from Muslims themselves; many of their own shops had put up such Christmas decorations, most of which have nothing to do with Christ's birth anyway (and Muslims also believe that he was born of a virgin). At the same time there appeared on television, at peak viewing time, a programme suggesting that Jesus was the result of a Roman soldier raping his mother Mary! A journalist commented that Christianity is now the only religion that can be openly mocked!

The media dare not ridicule Muhammad for fear of offending Muslim sensibilities, whereas it appears to be open season for mocking Christianity and even Christ himself (the film *Life of Brian* springs to mind). Why this huge disparity? One reason may be the widespread knowledge that Jesus taught non-resistance and non-retaliation to his followers ('turning the other cheek' has become part of our common language), so Christians are not a threat to be feared, whereas the term 'jihad' is widely assumed to include violence (we shall examine this more fully in Chapter 4) and thus does constitute a danger.

In concluding this impressionistic picture, I want to emphasise one thing. The prediction that inspired and underlies this book was not reached by any analysis of the facts and trends listed in this chapter. It was only after I had felt the premonition of an Islamic takeover that I began to realise the significance of these facts and trends and to investigate the current scene more thoroughly. From the information I have gathered, an even clearer picture seems to emerge.

A question surfaces. Will Islam take over by simple demographic change, by Muslims becoming so numerous they can take over with a simple majority, always possible in a democracy? Or will this be accelerated with increasing numbers of indigenous British converts embracing a faith that in many ways is alien to their temperament and tradition? Could Islam have a real appeal?

3

Its Appeal

A Christian friend of mine is a counsellor in a state school. He was delighted when a boy he was trying to help find a purpose in life told him he had become convinced there was a personal God in whom he could believe. To his surprise and disappointment this English boy told him some weeks later that he had become a Muslim. He was one of many thousands who have made the same choice.

Islam sprang out of an Arabic culture fourteen centuries ago, much of which it has retained, and is quite alien to traditional British culture, not least in matters of dress. Why are people in this country drawn to it? What is its appeal?

To find the answer we must engage in some 'Comparative Religion', a subject now taught in our state schools and which, as the name implies, compares one religion to another. In this case, we will compare and contrast Islam and Christianity.

Many years ago one of the first satirical shows on BBC television was David Frost's *That Was The Week That Was* (*TW3*). One programme presented a 'shoppers' guide to religion', in the style of the Consumers' Association and its *Which?* magazine. Points were awarded for benefits and subtracted for drawbacks. I forget which came out as the 'best buy'.

We too, will take the customer's viewpoint. The reader is invited to imagine he or she is a typical post-modern person looking for a spiritual dimension to life, convinced there must be a supreme being out there and wondering how best to relate. The quest begins with a look at the two religions with the largest number of followers.

The comparison will be based on impression rather than investigation, on the image picked up by the general public, who do not always appreciate the distinction between nominal attachment and genuine commitment, between what I would call Churchianity, as opposed to authentic Christianity.

Judged by simplistic criteria, Islam would seem to have considerable attraction. When compared to the public face of the Church, inevitably the established Church of England (though it no longer has more regular attendees than its Roman Catholic or Free Church counterparts, all these averaging under a million), Islam can easily be seen to be more recent, simple, easy, relevant, moral and masculine.

In making such generalised comparisons, allowance must be made for local exceptions, of which there may be a growing number. But the overall picture remains.

A RECENT RELIGION

In this regard, Islam has a twofold advantage, depending on whether a long-term or short-term meaning of 'recent' is considered. Either way, two widespread assumptions come into play – that later is better and newest is best.

Islam is a 'post-Christian' religion, Muhammad being born

600 years after Jesus. In fact it is the only major world religion to have appeared since Christianity began.

In so many other spheres of life, later editions of any product are expected to be improved versions and they usually are, benefiting from increased experience and improved understanding. It is hardly surprising if a consumer society has similar expectations in the matter of religion.

Islam thinks of itself in this way, acknowledging both Judaism and Christianity as its spiritual predecessors, by accepting a line of prophets from Adam to Jesus, but culminating in Muhammad. However, by completing and correcting all previous revelations, his message renders theirs obsolete and unnecessary. Indeed (as we shall see in Chapter 6), Muslims believe our Old and New Testaments have been so corrupted in transmission that they are no longer a trustworthy record of the teaching of earlier prophets, who are all believed to have been good Muslims, saying the same thing as the final messenger of God, Muhammad.

So Islam has an inherent self-assessment as the latest and best. It is therefore as psychologically difficult for Muslims to consider reverting to Jesus as for Christians to revert to Moses. Only an eccentric enthusiast for antiques would exchange the latest BMW car for a Model T Ford, the old 'tin Lizzie'.

There is a second way in which Islam has the advantage of a 'recent' image. It is relatively new to the British scene. While some may have known about it as a faith practised overseas or even had an encounter with the sprinkling of Muslim adherents in this country, general awareness belongs to the last few decades and only very recently have people considered it a viable and available alternative to the religious tradition of their upbringing or education.

We have already noted the search for new and meaningful

experiences in British contemporary culture, some into realms of 'spirituality'. It would be surprising if there were no interest in trying out this new arrival on the religious scene. Fads and fashions pursue the latest and newest.

A religion that was regarded as 'foreign' is increasingly familiar. One that was far away can now be next door. One that was alien to our way of life is becoming an acceptable part of it. It is now perfectly amenable to be a 'British Muslim', along with a growing proportion of the population, particularly in urban contexts (the label 'Muslim Briton' is unlikely to catch on, partly because the noun is rarely used but also because a noun carries more weight than an adjective).

So Islam is a 'new' religion, both historically and nationally. And there has always been an interest in novelty, especially in religion and philosophy. In ancient Greece, all the Athenians and the foreigners who lived there spent their time doing nothing but talking about and listening to the latest ideas, which gave Paul the chance to get a hearing for the new Christian faith (Acts 17:21). Islam is getting attention in the media for the same reason.

By contrast, the image of Christianity is old, even ancient. 'Old-fashioned', 'out of date', 'past its sell-by date', and other similar phrases reflect the opinion of many. At worst, services of worship are led by men wearing Roman dress, in Gothic buildings, with Elizabethan language (Art thou with it?), and Victorian music. Cathedrals are virtual museums, kept going by tourists' admission fees and better attended for musical and horticultural events than for praise and prayer.

For many, the Church is viewed with nostalgia for the past rather than hope for the future. Music still strikes a chord. The most requested item on the BBC's *Songs of Praise* is 'The old rugged cross'. The country still has a high proportion of ex-churchgoers and adults who went to Sunday school when they were children but 'have grown out of all that'.

Perhaps Christianity has been around too long to be appreciated, nearly two millennia. Familiarity breeds contempt. For many it's a case of 'tried and found wanting', though probably for more it's never even been tried. It simply belongs to the past, irrelevant to a generation living for the present and the future.

Perhaps Islam is the religion of the twenty-first century, as some of its followers claim. At any rate, it might be worth trying. And it has a number of other attractions, as well as being recent.

A SIMPLE RELIGION

Islam is simple enough to be grasped by all and sundry, and very quickly explained to others. Its creed could not be simpler, consisting of a single sentence combining the briefest references to two persons, one divine and the other human: 'There is no god but God (Allah) and Muhammad is his prophet (messenger)'! This is presented as a matter of fact rather then faith, with no introductory phrase like: 'I believe . . .'

Its scriptures are uncomplicated. Basically one book, a record of one man's 'recitations' (the meaning of the Arabic title, 'Al Quran' or 'Koran'). Of reasonable size, it has the same style throughout and is quite easily read through. It tells you what you need to know about God's will.

Its theology is straightforward and soon grasped. There is only one God (monotheism), who is in absolute control of our lives and whose will is irresistible (*Insh'allah*, 'God wills it', expresses a resigned acceptance, not far from fatalism).

But human beings, born in a state of innocence, are free to submit (Muslim means 'submitted one') to his will, or to rebel against it. On the day of reckoning, the creator from whom we came and to whom we are responsible will weigh up our good deeds against our bad deeds and decide our eternal destiny on the balance. However, being merciful and compassionate, he might show leniency and forgive some or all of the bad, though we cannot be sure of this until then. Paradise, a place of many pleasures including physical ones such as food, drink and sex, awaits those who pass; while endless torment in 'the Fire' awaits those who don't. There are spirit beings, some good (angels), who record our deeds and some bad (jinn, as mentioned earlier) who tempt us to do evil. Such are the basic 'fundamentals' believed by every Muslim.

Its terms of admission are the simplest of all. It is the easiest religion in the world to join. All that is required is the recital of the one-sentence creed in the presence of a witness.

By contrast, Christianity is much more complex and teaches much that is difficult to understand and accept. Its creeds are always much longer and mention five persons, three divine and two human, the latter a noble woman responsible for Christ's birth and an ignoble man responsible for his death. They combine a mixture of cosmological, historical, biological and ecclesiastical statements, often using obscure and archaic phrases ('very God of very God'). Though presenting facts, they are framed as a statement of faith, always beginning with: 'I believe . . .'

Its scriptures are far longer and more varied. Written by forty-plus authors over fourteen centuries, there are inevitably differences, not only in style and content but also of type (genre), including songs, proverbs, history, prediction, biography and letters. In fact, the Bible is not so much a book as a library of sixty-six books, divided into two collections: the Christian writings of the New Testament (about the same size as the Quran) and the Jewish writings of the Old Testament (four times the size), the latter incorporated because the God of Israel and the Father of Jesus are one and the same. It is a daunting task to read it through, not least because there are three-quarters of a million words. Many who try give up in the third book, Leviticus, because the gripping narrative of the first two books gives way to ancient legislation.

➡ Its theology appears quite irrational to many, much of it beyond the reach of natural reason. The creeds are invariably in three parts, each focusing on one of the three divine persons: Father, Son and Holy Spirit.

This immediately draws attention to its most distinctive element, unique among all world religions: that though there is only one God, there are at the same time three distinct persons called God, each conscious of himself and the others, yet so united in heart, mind and will that Christians never use the plural 'them' of God, only 'him'. This is neither strict monotheism (there is only one person we can call 'God') nor polytheism (belief in many gods, as in Hinduism) or even tritheism (three gods, which Muslims are prone to accuse Christians of). A unique word must be coined for this unique God: triunetheism. But a much simpler one has been in use for centuries: 'Trinity' (from tri-unity).

To believe that $1+1+1=1$ is mathematical nonsense (although $1\times1\times1=1$) but makes a lot of spiritual sense to the millions of Christians who have had a personal encounter with all three persons, yet find this compatible with their conviction that there can only be one God responsible for one uni-verse.

As if this is not enough to stretch our minds to their limit and beyond, there are beliefs about the second and third persons equally incredible and incomprehensible!

That Jesus was born of a virgin is extraordinary, though the Quran accepts this. What Muslims cannot accept is that he *chose* to be born as a man, having existed from all eternity as God's only Son. Christians call this the 'incarnation', which means a choice to become 'in flesh'.

Then there is the 'atonement', based on the insight that God cannot forgive sin without the compensation of a blood sacrifice, foreshadowed in the animal offerings of the Jews, but fulfilled in the crucifixion of Jesus at thirty-three, his execution adequate recompense for all the sins of the entire human race.

His resurrection three days later, 'reincarnated' into a new body but exactly the same person, has never happened to anyone else before or since. Two months later he floated up into space, without the aid of a rocket or protection of a spacesuit (we call it his 'ascension') and will one day return with the same body, not a day older.

The Holy Spirit is invisible but not impersonal. God himself takes up residence inside those who believe in his Son, making it possible for them to replicate his power and purity, the same 'gifts' and 'fruit' that he embodied, supernatural abilities and attributes otherwise forever beyond human reach.

Human beings are born sinners and cannot save themselves from the penalty, power and pollution of their self-centred rejection of divine revelation, which all have received through creation outside and conscience inside. Only by co-operation with Father, Son and Holy Spirit is salvation possible.

Christianity's terms of admission are more complex, precisely because they also are 'Trinitarian', involving repenting toward God the Father, believing in God the Son and receiving the Holy Spirit, together with being 'baptised' (immersed in water) in the name of all three (for a detailed explanation of these four steps, see the author's *The Normal Christian Birth*, Hodder & Stoughton, 1989).

Before closing this comparison, it is worth noting that at first sight Islam appears to be a much simpler and more acceptable version of Christianity, shorn of the dogma that present problems. There is more interest in duties than doctrines. Some will conclude that Islam is a simpler way of relating to the same God, without demanding such intellectual gymnastics.

And the 'do-it yourself' salvation of Islam, also found in every other religion, is much more amenable to the British way of thinking, from elite bodies like freemasonry and the public schools to the mythical 'man in the street' who is convinced he can be 'as good a Christian' without having anything to do with ecclesiastical association or doctrinal commitment. Practising self-help religion preserves pride, whereas admitting complete failure and acknowledging utter dependence is humiliating.

AN EASY RELIGION

We are now in the realm of 'ritual' requirements. Other than general behaviour, what has to be done to practise any particular religion? What spiritual activity am I expected to engage in?

Islam has five 'pillars', basic rules to be kept by all devout Muslims. They are well within everybody's capability. While they may be inconvenient, they are not impracticable and can easily be attained with some effort and discipline. As the Quran claims: 'Allah has not laid upon you a hardship in religion.'

The first is to recite the simple one-sentence creed regularly. The second is to say prayers to Allah at five set times every day and publicly with others each Friday. They do not take long but require a ritual washing of parts of the body beforehand. The third is to give alms to the poor (not the mullah or the mosque), a sum set at 2.5 per cent of income. The fourth is to fast every day during the month of Ramadan (during which Muhammad received his first revelations); this involves no eating or drinking (a real hardship in desert conditions!) between sunrise and sunset, mitigated by being able to do both as soon as it is dark. Fifth, to make a pilgrimage to Mecca in Arabia at least once in a lifetime, if possibly able to do so; it will involve walking round the sacred building called the *Ka'aba* seven times, making a sacrifice and going to a place outside the city to throw stones at the devil.

And that's it. The beauty of such demands lies in their being so clear and specific. They are not only comparatively easy to do but easy to know when they have been done. There is a satisfaction for those who have attained the standards required. It is a simple task to check one's self out and to know whether one is a 'good' Muslim. While requiring more than a casual commitment, the demands are not unreasonable.

By contrast, Christianity is much less satisfactory, or do I mean satisfying?

Praying, fasting and giving are all part of the devotional life, but there are no clear guidelines as to when or how, how often or how much, these are to be practised. Corporate worship and fellowship are clearly essential but when these should be observed and how they should be conducted is left open.

This lack of specifics can lead to two extreme responses. On the one hand, complacency, contentment with a minimal observance, a nominal adherence. On the other hand, a constant anxiety and sense of failure, often aggravated by preachers constantly exhorting their congregations to do more and better. This can explain why some Christians can get so miserable or are tempted to 'give it all up'.

In some ways it was easier to be a Jew under the law of Moses, with its more than 600 laws, summed up in the Ten Commandments. They knew they had to give a seventh of their time (sabbath) and a tenth of their income (tithe) to God. They knew what sacrifices were required for what sins.

Christians are not 'under' any of these rules, unless they are endorsed by Christ and his apostles. They are to be governed from the inside by the indwelling divine Spirit rather than from the outside by detailed legislation. But that requires a spirituality and sensitivity that takes time to develop and is the quest of a lifetime. Those who walk this way will be encouraged to press on by its results. But those who want to arrive at their goal quickly will be discouraged.

Churches have been tempted to revert to clear rules. Lent was a time of fasting like Ramadan. Tithing has been insisted upon (usually for the Church, not the poor). Attendance at public worship has been compulsory. Holy days have been earmarked (now they are holidays!) and festivals instituted (crowds attend Christmas Eve Communion). There is no trace of these in the New Testament and they are often a substitute for the responsibility of teaching people how to be led by the Spirit. And they encourage people who observe them to feel they have 'done their bit' for God.

Human nature prefers to be told exactly what to do than to have the responsibility of finding out for one's self what is pleasing to the Lord by getting to know him. A faith giving specific guidance about religious observance is at an advantage.

A REVERENT RELIGION

Anyone who has witnessed public prayers in a mosque will have been struck by the seriousness with which they are conducted. The sight of rows of men of all ages and ranks standing equally together and then prostrating themselves before God, their foreheads touching the ground, is a sight not quickly forgotten.

Reverence is a mixture of respect and awe, which cannot take things lightly or casually. In the Muslim case, this extends to their scripture, which is kept on a high shelf in the home and never held below waist level (they are shocked to see Christians drop a Bible on the floor), and to the one who brought it to them. They will not hear a word against him, are jealous for his name and reputation and forbid any pictorial representation of him in books, plays or films. Blasphemy of any kind is deserving of death.

Fear is an essential ingredient of reverence. Muslims fear God. They take his future judgement of all human beings very seriously indeed and are as convinced of the reality of hell as of heaven, believing that any Muslim could finish up in 'the Fire'. They are, indeed, a God-fearing people and have pointed out the lack of this in Western civilisation and therefore an important contribution Islam can bring to British society.

By contrast, the fear of the Lord has largely disappeared from contemporary Christianity. Though spoken about many times in the Bible, in both Old and New Testaments, it is hardly mentioned, much less experienced in churches today. Our worship is increasingly informal and even casual. A friend of mine put it like this: 'We seem to be worshipping God all-matey, not God almighty.' At worst, it can be little different from a session at a disco, with its band, lead and backing singers and a platform covered with wires and amplifiers, to say nothing of the heavy drumbeat setting the rhythm to which the congregation can move and shake. Kneeling is out, even to receive communion. Seating must be comfortable. Dress down rather than up; after all, it is the weekend.

One reason for the disparity is that Muslims go to the mosque for one purpose: to do what pleases Allah. Whereas declining congregations in a consumer society can become obsessed with the idea of 'user-friendly' services, deliberately aimed to please people and getting close to an entertaining performance. This may be acceptable and even advisable in an evangelistic event, but has a damaging effect on worship.

But there is a theological reason as well. To those fed on an unbalanced diet with an excess of God's love and a deficiency of his righteousness, he is no longer feared because he is no longer a threat. A God of 'love', interpreted sentimentally rather than scripturally, would not hurt a fly, much less send anybody to hell. Whatever happened to: 'Let us . . . so worship God acceptably with reverence and awe, for our God is a consuming fire' (Hebrews 12:28–9, quoting Deuteronomy 4:24)?

The answer is that if he is only presented as a comforting father (more like a grandfather!), people will never have the feeling of being close to an erupting volcano or a raging bush fire.

This absence of the fear of the Lord, which is the very 'beginning of wisdom', is reflected in our manner of life as much as our worship, in declining moral standards as well as our devotions. Which brings us to another comparison and contrast:

A MORAL RELIGION

The moral standards of Islam may be quite different from ours but their popular image is that they are 'strict' in applying them. Muslims are as against immorality (as they define it) as idolatry (the two usually go together, as the Old Testament history clearly reveals).

Nor do they shrink from applying discipline within their families and communities when the rules are flouted. They are enforced with the sanction of severe punishment. The penalties for adultery, theft and murder are well known, including loss of limb and life. And it works: stealing is rare in Arabia.

But the ultimate sanction is in the next world, not this. Muslims are convinced of the reality of hell-fire and the possibility of everlasting torment is as real for them as the promised delights of Paradise. Future prospects provide effective motivation for behaviour in this life.

They are generally disgusted with the moral decadence of Western society, despising the obsession with sex, drugs and drink (alcohol is forbidden to them until the wine of Paradise). Such permissiveness is totally alien to them, creating tension in immigrant families when they see their children corrupted by their peer groups and the media.

Nor do they hesitate to ascribe this state of affairs to the failure and even inherent weakness of Christianity. Of course, we need to remember they think in collective terms, that everyone born in a Muslim country is a Muslim and therefore everyone born in the 'Christian West' is a Christian. Nor is it easy to persuade them otherwise, as I learned one Christmas Day in 1960. As an RAF chaplain in the Middle East, I took a bunch of recent converts away from the camp and its heavy drinking binge. We went fishing in an Arab boat. One of the

Arabs told me he thought Christianity a *mush tamam* (not good) religion because 'you celebrate your founder's birthday by getting drunk', which they would consider an insult to Muhammad if they did the same.

We can try and defend Christianity against such charges by pointing out that Western nations are only nominally 'Christian' and genuine committed Christians are a religious minority. But has the Church no responsibility for the state of the British nation? And does the Church itself preach and practise consistently higher standards than the surrounding society? Actually, the Church is regularly criticised for failing to give clear moral guidance and compromising its own inherited traditions. This complaint is particularly directed at the established Church because of its privileged position in public life. Yet its pride in being a latitudinarian 'umbrella', welcoming a wide variety of theological and ethical opinions for the sake of a national image of unity, is compromised within as well as seeming to be over-eager to accommodate its position to social trends. Homosexual relationships and consecutive polygamy (as many wives as you like, as long as they are one at a time, as distinct from simultaneous polygamy) are now accepted by society in general, so the Church follows suit by accepting gay applicants into membership, even ministry, and by marrying divorcees. Paedophilia is still frowned upon by most, so the Church is still embarrassed when it is exposed among its clergy. Instead of leading society upwards into a holier and happier lifestyle, the Church often seems to be following society downwards, but dragging its heels behind everyone else.

More seriously, hell-fire is no longer thought of as a possible threat, even by evangelical preachers! Conditional immortality or annihilationism, the belief that sinners eventually simply cease to exist, either at death or after judgement, is now widely held. That this alternative is not likely to motivate good or deter bad living is shown by the fact that those who believe it don't preach it. After all, a man is not likely to abandon a life of sin, vice or crime because he will one day go to sleep and never wake up again. It is the possibility of paying for it all in terms of endless anguish with no hope of escape that is likely to lead to repentance. Sophisticated talk about fear being a poor motive needs to remember that all we Christians know about hell came from the lips of Jesus, who had no hesitation in using it, supremely in the 'Sermon on the Mount'. Even more disturbing, he addressed almost all his warnings about its horrors to his own disciples! Christians need to fear hell as much, if not more, than outright 'sinners' (for a full explanation of this point, see the author's *The Road to Hell*, Hodder & Stoughton, 1992). If there is no fear of hell inside the Church there is not likely to be much outside. Too many Christians are too complacent, having been assured by evangelists and pastors that a single profession of faith, expressed in a brief 'sinner's prayer', guarantees them a place in heaven. The unbiblical cliché: 'Once saved, always saved' has given them a doubtful feeling of security (I examine this presumption in: *Once Saved, Always Saved?*, Hodder & Stoughton, 1996). We all need to recall that: 'without holiness no-one will see the Lord' (Hebrews 12:14).

As our communities plunge further into moral anarchy, there may well be a backlash, from the resulting damage and danger, a demand for a return to clear standards, applied in 'law and order'. This could be a decisive factor in future elections and lead to autocratic government by one party or even one person. Frustrated people may well turn to religion for moral inspiration and authority, seeking some security for themselves and their families. If that happens, Islam looks more likely to gain a hearing than the Church as it is.

A MALE RELIGION

This comparison may come as a surprise, but it is very relevant to the future of religion and, indeed, of society in general. Whether we like it or not, and feminists definitely don't, the fact is that the vast majority of decisions shaping our life together are taken by men, in almost all spheres of influence – political, commercial, industrial, cultural and so on. From this very obvious fact we can infer that the religion that will have most impact and influence will be the one that will command the loyalty of men who have social responsibilities.

Islam is a religion for men, who are quite unembarrassed, even proud, to profess and practise their faith in public. Mosques are packed with male congregations, each taking a very active role in worship, from beginning to end. And it is for men in their prime as well as the young and the elderly. Nor are they ashamed to mention God in private conversation or public speeches.

And it is very much a 'lay' religion. While there are imams and mullahs, most ministry and especially missionary activity is carried out by what churches would call the 'lay members'. It has been largely through travelling merchants that Islam has spread through East and West Africa, men going about their daily business but not leaving their religion behind in the mosque each Friday.

By contrast, Christianity has an increasingly feminine image. Churches have much in common with Titanic's life-boats: women and children first. Few churches have as many men as women in the congregations (in the last two parish churches I have spoken in, the ratio was 1:5). Leadership is more and more in the hands of women, especially since ordination was extended to them, first by Free Churches and then by the Church of England (the then Archbishop of Canterbury arguing that 'the Church must be credible to contemporary society'). We shall soon see women bishops and ultimately one holding the see of Canterbury. For the first time in history, the Church of Scotland has more women elders than men. Even the remaining male clergy tend to have a feminine personality profile (according to research into 155 Anglican ordinands conducted by the Rev. Leslie Francis of Trinity College, Carmarthen, 97 female ordinands had 'a characteristically masculine profile', while the men tended to be feminine in social attitudes).

The churches have succumbed to the pressures of feminism and political correctness by commissioning an 'inclusivist' version of the Bible, in which God is 'Father-Mother' and Jesus is not the 'Son of Man', but the 'Child of Human Being'. One witty reviewer spotted a glaring inconsistency when he commented: 'The devil must be laughing her head off.' A life-sized sculpture of a crucifix has been hung in a cathedral, with the figure of Christ totally nude and totally female. The BBC daily morning service has used prayers to our Mother in heaven and referred to God as a goddess: 'She'.

At the domestic level, wives are frequently more religious than their husbands, and mothers rather than fathers pass it on to their children. Matriarchy, the female leadership of the family, was relatively rare in Western society, but is now rampant. Sociologists in Australia have had to coin a new word for its dominance there: matriduxy.

Arabic culture, from which Islam emanated, was patriarchal, as most other cultures have been until recently.

Judaism and Christianity both arose in the same Middle East milieu. The New Testament clearly puts the responsibility for leadership on the shoulders of men, from Jesus' choice of the twelve apostles, to the churches' choice of elders. However, this is now seen as 'cultural conditioning' due to social mores in those days and no longer applicable today (for a discussion of this, see my *Leadership is Male*, 1988, now published by Bethel Books).

This section would not be complete without a reference to the Islamic attitude to women, which is probably already in the reader's mind. It is true that in the Quran there is gender discrimination based on Muhammad's teaching that women are inferior to men, their legal testimony of less value and their inheritance rights halved. The insistence on complete covering of the body is also irksome to modern society. The phrase 'second-class citizens' is freely used in this context.

Yet against this is the fact that there are more female than male converts to Islam and not all through marrying into it. One striking example is the conversion of leaders of the 'Greenham Common' protest camp outside the American nuclear airbase in Berkshire. Others have gone on record as preferring to be 'covered up' since they no longer have to compete in the sex object stakes but find they are 'accepted as persons' in their own right. Wives have welcomed the greater stability and security of Muslim family life. Deep down, most women want and welcome manly men who will take their responsibilities of provision and protection for their families seriously.

We must summarise this extended chapter.

We have tried to put ourselves in the shoes of a non-believer feeling the need for a religious dimension to life and deciding which of the available options to sample. In a consumer society such as Britain's now is, the choice is not likely to be made on grounds of objective truth but on subjective satisfaction. 'What suits me' is likely to be decisive.

We have tried to show that Islam has a lot going for it in this market. Its public image, in Britain at any rate, has its attraction, when compared with its main competitor, Christianity. It would not therefore be surprising if an increasing number of British people adopted this faith and life.

Readers may well have concluded by now that I am encouraging this by comparing Christianity with Islam so unfavourably. But that has not been my intention. Rather I have tried to help Christians to see themselves as others can see them, which is very much part of *The Challenge of Islam to Christians*.

But comparisons can cut both ways and there is an unfavourable side to Islam, a 'downside' to use a current term, enough to make a potential convert pause to consider their intention very carefully. To this we must now address ourselves.

4

Its Essence

Islam is the easiest religion in the world to get into. All one has to do is recite aloud the basic creed of a few words. At the same time it is the hardest to get out of. Such 'apostasy' is treated as a crime, an act of treason carrying the death penalty (as it did in Britain until recently).

Why should a spiritual decision be regarded as a criminal matter? The answer will take us to the heart of that religion, to its very essence. Before proceeding with the explanation, we need to mention three basic sources to be used.

First, the Quran (English 'Koran'). Muslims are, like Jews and Christians, people of a Book. Theirs is smaller than the Bible; as we've noted, roughly the size of the New Testament. It is a compilation of revelations received and 'recited' by one man over a few decades, written down by others and edited into a definitive volume after his death.

Second, the 'Hadith'. This is a collection of recollections rather than recitations; things that Muhammad said and did, in addition to his direct revelations. In this are found Allah's ninety-nine names, Muhammad's ride to heaven from Jerusalem and mention of the death penalty for adultery and apostasy.

Third, the 'Shariah' law. Based on both the Quran and the Hadith, this contains Islamic legislation for Muslim communities, local and national. As the proportion of Muslims grows in any country, so does the pressure to establish this code of conduct over all.

From these three authoritative sources a picture emerges, which presents a much less attractive aspect than that portrayed in the previous chapter. From a Christian point of view, there is a real downside, even apart from doctrinal disagreement. It is radically different in its scope and application:

A TOTAL RELIGION

I avoided using the adjectives 'holistic' and 'totalitarian', both being too emotive, though in opposite directions, one being acceptable and the other unacceptable. The word 'total' serves the purpose of highlighting two major characteristics.

On the one hand, Islam claims the whole life of the individual. Rules cover every activity, from the sublime to the mundane. This may be illustrated by the injunction in the Quran to pray towards Mecca and the one in the Hadith to turn away from Mecca when defecating or urinating. Every aspect of life is regulated, from money to marriage, diet to dress.

From one point of view, Christians can applaud this, believing that holiness must extend to the whole of life. 'If he's not Lord of all, he's not Lord at all.' But they are also aware of the danger of legalism and outward conformation. They know the real secret is to be led by the Holy Spirit from the inside.

On the other hand, Islam claims the whole life of the community as well. It is here that we touch its very essence. It sees society as a 'theocracy', government by God, as Allah's will for the political as well as the personal sphere.

In this, Islam may be compared to Israel in the Old Testament. The Mosaic law is not dissimilar to the Muslim law. Capital punishment for adultery or blasphemy is an obvious example. Ceremonial and criminal laws jostle each other, with no demarcation between spiritual, moral and social requirements. Sins against God and crimes against society are treated in the same way, as infringements of the law. When God rules a nation, his revealed will supplies the body of legislation. There is no need for debate or democracy, just agents of enforcement and sanctions for the disobedient. All that is required of citizens in a theocracy is 'submission' (the meaning of 'Muslim') to the will of God revealed through his prophet(s).

Christians have discerned a different emphasis in the New Testament where the respective claims of Caesar and God are clearly distinguished. The state government is seen as a servant of God, ordained by him for the maintenance of peace and order, the restraint of evil and punishment of evil-doers, if necessary by the use of force and the taking of life (Romans 13:1–5 is the classic statement). But the mission of the Church is very different and separate, using spiritual rather than 'carnal' weapons (John 18:36; 2 Corinthians 10:4).

Indeed, church history highlights the danger when Church and State are united, as they were from the 'conversion' of the Emperor Constantine onwards. From this 'Christendom', in which the later Popes held both 'keys', came the infamous Crusades and Inquisition. Even Luther and Calvin fell into the same trap, leading to bloodshed in Germany and Geneva. When the Christian religion is 'established' by law, inhumanity and injustice invariably result. America is a unique example of the separation of Church and State, but its 'Founding Fathers' insisted on this to prevent any Christian denomination from gaining 'Established' monopoly and would have been horrified to see their statutes used to promote an atheistic stance.

In Islam, there is no difference between 'church' and 'state'. In essence it must ultimately be the established religion in any country, its values and standards imposed on the whole population by law. There is no distinction between sin, vice and crime. All are legal offences.

Muslims can never be content with individual conversions to their faith. They want to see communities 'submitting' to Allah's will as well. Islam is therefore far more than a personal religion. It is a legal, social, political and even military force for change, wherever its adherents are. It can be fully practised only where Shariah law is rigidly imposed and obeyed.

From this most basic and important core, many other serious implications follow.

A TERRITORIAL RELIGION

According to Muslim teaching, the world is divided into two territories: the sphere or land of Peace – Dar ul Salaam (land of peace, i.e. which is under Shariah law) and the sphere or land of War – Dar ul Harb (land of war, not yet under Islam, not yet under Allah's control). Success in mission is not primarily seen in terms of individuals converting but in terms of countries submitting to Allah. Muslims are now the majority in forty-five countries in Africa and Asia. Even where they are in a minority, they exercise a controlling influence out of proportion to their number, as in 'middle' Nigeria.

If Islamic territory is attacked it must be defended by military force, as in all other cases where national boundaries are infringed. Even more important, land that has belonged to Allah in the past and been lost to the 'infidel' must be retaken by force. In both cases, Muslims are allowed to sign peace treaties in cases where their forces face superior foes, but these must be abrogated as soon as they have built up sufficient strength for a successful attack and always within a maximum period of ten years.

All this explains why Israel is such an offence to the Arab world, especially since the Israeli government has reclaimed Jerusalem (the third holiest city of Islam since Muhammad had his vision of ascending to heaven from it) as their 'eternal capital'. It lies behind the declared radical intention to 'drive' Israel into the sea and the widespread loathing of Americans for their support for Israel, enabling her to stay in her 'promised land'.

We also need to recall how much of Europe was once the 'land of Islam'. Muslim forces came through Spain and France as far as Poitiers and later through the Balkans to the gates of Vienna.

AN IMPERIAL RELIGION

Muslims not only have a duty to defend Islamic territory or retake former Islamic land; they are also committed to taking new territory, whether by invasion or infiltration. Since 'there is no god but Allah', they cannot rest until the whole world is restored to him. Since he created it, the world belongs to him by right and he has given the responsibility for getting it back to his followers. The goal is quite clear, though the means of reaching it may vary, from physical to mental persuasion.

In other words, Islam is a missionary religion, intent on bringing all the nations of the world under Allah's rule. It is striking, however, that its spread is often achieved by 'lay' rather than 'clerical' members. For example, it was carried down the east coast of the African continent by traders and sailors.

Christianity too, is a missionary religion, intent on taking its gospel 'to the ends of the earth'. But its mandate from Christ is to make disciples of all ethnic groups rather than attempt to get governmental control. It has often relied on 'professional' missionaries, paid to spread the faith, and it has sometimes entered a country under the cover and protection of imperial expansion and colonisation, in India, for example. But many have gone without such support and protection, at considerable and often supreme sacrifice. When true to itself, Christianity refuses to use force, choosing to die rather than kill. Jesus committed his followers to a policy of non-resistance. The end does not justify any means.

Islam is more than missionary. Because 'church' and 'state' are identical, it is an imperial religion as well. Since most empires have been extended by the use of some kind of force, sometimes commercial but usually military, we need to ask how far this is also true of Islam, as it seeks to extend its territory to the whole world. Global ambitions invariably lead to martial aggression.

A MILITANT RELIGION

Most Christians believe that national states are permitted to use 'the sword' to maintain internal stability and to defend themselves against external threats. However, they believe the latter must fulfil the qualifications of a 'just war'; that is, a conflict that can be 'justified' on moral grounds.

However, when church and state become one entity, as in medieval Christendom and Islam throughout its history, a new concept emerges – the 'holy war', justified on spiritual grounds and usually regarded as a 'crusade' against rival faiths.

It is time to look at the meaning of what Islam calls a 'jihad', very widely assumed to refer to such a 'holy war', the use of physical force and arms in a religious conflict.

Since the suicidal terrorist attacks on New York and Washington on 11 September 2001, Muslims living in the Western world have been at pains to disassociate themselves from this 'extremism', to portray Islam as a peace-loving religion and to interpret 'jihad' in spiritual rather than physical terms. This apologetic would be more convincing if they had also condemned the same tactics being used by Palestinians against Israelis and the slaughter of Christians in Indonesia, Sudan and Nigeria. From the silence one can only assume that they believe those atrocities are justified.

So what does 'jihad' actually mean and what range of conflict does it cover? This is an important question because of its prominence in Muslim faith and practice. It has even been called 'the sixth pillar of Islam'; that is, an essential responsibility placed on all who seek to submit to the will of Allah.

The basic meaning of the word is 'struggle' or 'effort'. And in context, it means the struggle against evil forces, supremely the arch-devil Satan (*Shaitan* in Arabic).

Of course, this includes the internal struggle. There is a jihad of the tongue, the effort required to speak about the faith to others; the jihad of the hand, the effort required to do good deeds; the jihad of the heart, the effort required to resist temptation. We may summarise this as the call to struggle with infidelity in one's self.

What about the struggle with infidelity in others?

Unbelievers are called 'infidels' in the Quran. At one point, Muslims are exhorted to 'fight, fight, fight the infidel'. But the Arabic word is actually 'kill, kill, kill'. This is far from being an isolated exhortation.

Historically, the sword played a major role in the spread of Islam. Muhammad himself was involved in numerous battles. The citizens of Mecca defeated him twice but finally surrendered when his forces became superior. Arab fighters swept through Arabia and the Middle East, into northern Africa, western Asia and southern Europe, leaving in their wake an 'established' Islam to replace all other faiths.

Even today, violence is justified by identifying perceived enemies as demonic agents. Israel is 'little Satan' and America is 'big Satan'. Both can therefore be legitimately destroyed in the name of the God who is greater – *'Allah akbar'* has become a battle cry during such attacks.

However, we need to recognise what some have called 'a struggle for the soul of Islam', between the 'militants' and the 'modernists', the latter limiting 'jihad' to the inward struggle against evil. We shall look at this in greater detail in the next chapter and attempt to assess which interpretation is likely to prevail.

Meanwhile, we note that to a Muslim 'peace' is more likely to mean the exclusive establishment of Islamic rule than the tolerant co-existence of different religions.

AN EXCLUSIVE RELIGION

In its concentrated form, Islam is intolerant of all other religions. Saudi Arabia, its heartland, with the two holy cities of Mecca and Medina, is the supreme example. No other faith can be seen to have a place. The only religious buildings are all mosques. Police enforce cessation of employment on Fridays so that all may attend prayers.

—The Quran does not mention other world religions such as Hinduism, Buddhism or Shintoism. Muhammad never directly encountered them. But his attitude to the indigenous polytheism of his native Arabia may be taken as an indication of what he would have said about them.

Given the inherent conviction that Islam will one day be the religion of the entire world, all nations having come under the rule of Allah, it is hardly surprising that there should be a negative attitude to other faiths. Presumably, they will all die out or be killed off as Islam advances around the globe.

Exclusive claims inevitably lead to intolerance, in attitude if not in action. The Quran has been used to present infidels (unbelievers) with the stark choice: convert or die, submit or perish. The Catholic Inquisition has had its counterpart in Muslim history.

However, the attitude of Islam to Judaism and Christianity is in a different category and must be viewed separately. Muhammad had direct contact with both Jews and Christians, synagogues and churches. He respected both, not least because they preceded himself in holding firmly to a mono-theistic faith in a polytheistic society. This persistence sprang from being 'People of the Book', scriptures stemming from a succession of the one God's messengers, whom Muhammad recognised as genuine 'prophets' (though he regarded the record of their revelations in Old and New Testaments to have been dangerously corrupted).

This sympathetic regard is reflected in the earlier recita-tions (or suras) in the Quran (confusingly, they are placed later in the Quran). They come from the days when the prophet and his followers prayed towards Jerusalem and Saturday was the holy 'sabbath'. But the Jews did not accept

Muhammad as their final 'prophet', nor did Christians as their final 'apostle', virtually refusing to add his revelations to their scriptures. The tone of his comments changes in later suras (confusingly, they come earlier in the Quran). The climax is reached with a command not to have friendships with Jews or Christians. Attacks on Jewish communities began and persecution of Christians has continued to this day. There are now no synagogues or churches in the whole of Arabia.

However, there have been some concessions to Jews and Christians, perhaps because of a lingering sympathy with their monotheism. The choice for the pagan infidel, 'convert or die', has been modified in their case to include a third option. Provided they are willing to live under Shariah law, their personal faith is tolerated. But they cannot have full civic rights. Classed as having *Dhimmi* status, they are relegated to permanent second-class citizenship. In addition, they are subject to a special tax, which in practice is little different from a protection racket. From time to time, special identifying clothes (often yellow) have had to be worn, exposing them to public humiliation. And any propagation of their faith is strictly forbidden.

Such, then, are some of the implications of this 'total' religion. But the question remains as to whether all Muslims are equally convinced about them. Is there not a considerable variety of views and attitudes, particularly between those who live in Islamic countries and those who are minorities within Western culture? Are we not hearing contradictory propaganda, especially since the '9–11' event? Who are we to believe? Which is 'true' (i.e. real) Islam? To this dilemma we now turn.

5

Its Variety

It is perhaps inevitable that any religion will develop a variety of beliefs and behaviour patterns, since it is practised and propagated by a diversity of fallible human beings. To its foundational standards, often embodied in 'sacred' scriptures, there will be added a multiplicity of traditions, leading in turn to differences of interpretation and application of the original 'revelation', which then cause division by disagreement.

This has all happened to Christianity. In a simplistic analysis, we can distinguish three kinds of division, which we can label as structure, stream or strength in type.

STRUCTURE

Often focusing on the issue of loyalty to leadership, this kind of division is the most obvious. Most are aware that there are different 'denominations'. The word means no more than a label that distinguishes one group of Christians from another, though to the name are quickly added structures, centralised headquarters, publications, representative gatherings, clerical hierarchies and, above all, corporate finance.

Though there were 'regional' Churches quite early in its history (Coptic, Syriac, Ethiopian, etc.), the first major split was in 1054, between the Eastern Orthodox and Western Catholic. Ostensibly over one small clause in the creed, the real issue was probably political rather than theological – whether the old capital Rome or the new capital Constantinople (later reverting to its original name, Byzantium) was to decide what Christians believe. The other huge division came some five centuries later, between Catholics and Protestants, the latter divided from the beginning and subsequently splitting into myriad bodies. Unity and disunity seem to relate to the question of who leads. Catholics have one pope, Orthodox have a few patriarchs (Greek, Russian, etc.), while Protestants follow a multitude of preachers and pastors, even prone to building churches around one man's ministry.

STREAM

These divisions often focus on the practice of piety. Different streams cut right across the denominational divisions, creating a kind of cross-coloured 'tartan' pattern (Scots will understand!). Three examples will suffice:

The 'sacramental' stream, sometimes called 'high church', puts great emphasis on 'holy communion' (or 'mass') as the central act of Christian worship, accompanied by altars, priests, vestments and incense, all of which are more reminiscent of Old Testament 'temple' services than the New Testament 'synagogue' type.

The 'evangelical' stream, sometimes called 'low church',

puts more emphasis on the 'Word' than the sacraments, giving the reading and preaching of the Bible more prominence.

The 'charismatic' or 'Pentecostal' stream seeks the less formal and more spontaneous worship that allows the Holy Spirit to take more initiative, emphasising the gifts that can be exercised by any, not just the priest or preacher.

While some have become separate structures, most remain within existing denominations, and links between them are federal rather than executive.

STRENGTH

The issue here is submission to original standards, especially in Scripture. Broadly speaking (very!), three 'levels' are discernible, though they fade into each other.

Many are 'nominal' Christians. A recent poll in the UK found 74 per cent, three-quarters of the population, professing to be 'Christian'. This figure needs to be taken with caution, even scepticism. For many it's a way of saying they're not Muslim, Hindu or Buddhist. For others it's the church they stay away from rather than go to – except for such rites of passage as birth, marriage and death (hatches, matches and dispatches!), to which some add puberty (confirmation). Others give token attention to Christian festivals such as Christmas and Easter. Probably the majority have no personal relationship with the Trinitarian God but regard Christianity as being generally decent yourself and kind to others. It is largely a cultural hangover from the past.

Then there are 'liberal' Christians who are willing to adjust their standards of belief and behaviour to the contemporary mores of society today. Parts of the Bible are regarded as 'unscientific' if treated as fact, and are to be taken as myth, faction or even fiction, containing moral and spiritual but not historical truth. Its ethical demands are seen as 'culturally conditioned' and free to be adapted as felt necessary. The 'kingdom of God' is interpreted as a socio-political programme.

Finally there are 'conservative' Christians who take the Bible very seriously, literally where they believe the authors mean their words to be taken literally. Scripture is for them the final authority in all matters of belief and behaviour with no liberty to change it. They are derided for being 'fundamentalist', a word used frequently by others but rarely by themselves. It is almost a synonym for 'bigot' or 'fanatic'. In a relativist age it is offensive to be dogmatic or to claim any absolute values and standards that apply to everybody.

I have begun this chapter with a sketch of the variety within Christianity for two reasons. First, to remind Christians of what a divided front we present to people of other faiths, including Muslims, and nowhere more obviously than in Jerusalem, the third holiest city of Islam. It is a scandal, adding an unnecessary offence to the gospel. It was neither the intention of Jesus nor the object of his intercession (John 17:20–3). A growing sense of guilt over this led some of the more liberal church bodies to form the World Council of Churches in 1948. Typically, the more conservative formed a rival International Council of Christian Churches in the same year! But there is increasing co-operation, especially at grass-roots level.

Islamic apologists have not been slow to point out many divisions as a symptom of the weakness of the faith we hold. Against this they have set the universal brotherhood (the *ummah*) of those who have embraced Islam. On first impressions, they have a point. There is an apparent unity, even uniformity, in the worship of all mosques, partly due to an insistence on the Arabic language and the standardised postures and ritual.

But Islam is not a homogeneous, monolithic entity. For one thing, it has no centralised headquarters controlling its worldwide practice. Mecca is only the focus of its devotion and pilgrimage. There is diversity within its unity.

So the second reason for beginning with Christian divisions is simply to point to all the same kinds of divergence that have appeared within Islam, though this is not generally realised.

There are divisions of *structure*, based on loyalty to different leaders. Muhammad did not anticipate his death, so made no arrangements whatever for a successor to take over his leadership of the movement. Since he was the last 'prophet', they would be given the title of 'caliph'. Perhaps inevitably, there was a division of opinion as to whether this responsibility should fall on one of his close colleagues or one of his relatives (Arab tribal chiefs came from family dynasties and national rulers in Arab countries still do, as in the Saudi kingdom of Arabia and the Hashemite kingdom of Jordan).

So were born the two main 'denominations' within Islam, the Sunni and the Shiite. Each would develop its own traditions. And there would be real tension between them, leading to violence and bloodshed, which continues to this day. The horrific wars between Iraq (Sunni) and Iran (Shiite, the only whole Islamic nation of this persuasion) is one example, and the civil strife within Iraq itself between the Baghdad mid-region (Sunni) and the swampy south around Basra (Shiite) is another.

And there are smaller Islamic groupings, usually gathered around a leadership succession. The Aga Khan's is one such.

There are also *streams* within these larger divisions and cutting across them. The best known is the Sufi. It has been recently called 'the charismatic wing' of Islam, its worship being more lively and joyful, even ecstatic. It would be more accurate to describe it as the 'mystical' stream in Islam. Significantly, it arose out of the eastern spread of Islam, as it encountered other world religions of mystical type. Such piety seeks immediate communion with deity and ultimate union with deity, in which the self is absorbed into the one (or ones) worshipped. The Islamic version is not content with knowing about God's will from the past, but seeks to know him himself in the present. Christianity is able to offer precisely what Sufis seek, but there are some real hurdles to overcome before they can accept it.

There are differences of *strength*, especially in the realm of submission to their own scriptures. There is a real difference between the liberal Muslim, with a flexible attitude to the sacred text and willing to adapt its interpretation and application to the modern world, and the conservative Muslim, with a fixed attitude and determined to apply it rigidly to himself and others. And of course, there are many nominal Muslims as well. Let's begin with them.

'Nominal' Muslims maintain a semblance of their religion, more for reasons of cultural identity than theological conviction. Traditions like diet and dress, fasting and festival, survive, while others – prayer five times a day, for example – may lapse. Taboos against alcohol and usury (lending or borrowing money with interest) may be overlooked, particularly among the wealthier. And there is increasing peer pressure on the young generation to depart further from their upbringing. The proportion of nominalism is obviously greater where Muslims are a minority in an increasingly secular environment.

The same is true of 'liberal' Muslims, especially those who have fled from countries controlled by conservatives imposing Shariah law, as in Iran and Afghanistan. Immigrants in Western society, legal and illegal, welcome the freedom available in democratic countries, even if it means accepting the privatisation of their religion; that is, limiting its observance to personal and domestic spheres, without attempting to impose it on public policy in any way. This does involve a radical reinterpretation of Islamic scriptures, usually by treating them metaphorically or allegorically instead of literally. Jihad is limited to inward, spiritual, individual 'struggle' rather than a military exercise. It is part of liberal propaganda that Islam is a peaceable religion, in spite of its long history of extension by aggression (in this connection it needs to be remembered that Muslims are permitted to deceive 'infidels'). Liberal Muslims are more willing to engage in dialogue with other faiths and be regarded as part of the 'faith community', in common opposition to godless society.

'Conservative' Muslims take their scriptures and traditions much more seriously, much more literally. Those opposed to them have used epithets such as 'extremist', 'radical' and 'fundamentalist'. One of them recently responded by saying that all true Muslims are fundamentalist, in that they hold firmly to the fundamentals of their faith. To be true to the Quran does involve a commitment to the vision of Islam as the established and exclusive religion of every nation, bringing all into submission to the will of Allah. Privatisation is a dangerous distortion. Physical violence is an acceptable policy to defend the cause and territory of Allah or even to attack his enemies.

The big question is which of these three groups will prevail as the major influence. Since the terrorist attacks of 11

September 2001, the Western world (mainly Europe and North America) has been wrestling with this crucial dilemma. President Bush and Prime Minister Blair have pinned their hopes and based their policy on a liberal ascendancy, at least among Muslims living in Western society, and a decline of the conservative element in their midst. However, there are factors that could prove this assumption to be somewhat naive.

One is a matter of simple statistics. Islam is the fastest-growing religion, in Western countries, as in the rest of the world. This is by immigration as well as conversion, but mainly by a much higher birth-rate than other families. As so often, Israel reflects the wider democratic trends; in the foreseeable future there will be more Palestinian Arabs than Israeli Jews within its borders.

With increasing numbers comes greater power under democracy. Political pressure is already being felt in Britain, in local and national government. Exemption from British law, where it is in conflict with Islamic practice, is being successfully applied for, while political correctness favours positive discrimination of minorities. Examples range through inheritance, marriage, education and even mortgages. After exemption comes alteration, to bring national law more into line with Shariah law.

The acid test of Islamic intentions is what happens when the followers are in the majority and have enough voting power to take over a democratic country. There are enough examples to give some indication. The facts are not encouraging for the survival of pluralism. To take just one example, Turkey was founded as a secular republic just after World War One, but recent elections revealed a lurch to the religious right. In the former British colony of Malaysia there is a delicate balance between Westernised liberals and

Middle-Easternised conservatives, so the future could go either way.

Stronger religious convictions have a tendency to prevail over weaker ones. Uncompromised principles attract greater loyalty, especially if supported by negative emotions.

One very significant factor is a widespread hatred of Western political policy and contempt for its moral decadence, both of which are assumed to reflect 'Christian' values. This attitude is most pronounced in Muslim countries in the Middle East. It is not unrelated to British (and French) occupation of their countries in the first half of the twentieth century. It is exacerbated by the cultural imperialism of America in the second half of that century (the author has visited Arabian villages without piped water but a plentiful supply of Coca-Cola!). But the loathing focuses on the establishment of the State of Israel and the American support that has made its survival possible over numerous conflicts with surrounding Arab states. It is regarded as an invasive intrusion into the heartland of Muslim territory of Western democracy and decadence, both seen as an affront to Allah. A violent jihad is therefore seen as morally justified and the present *intifada* (uprising) is not likely to end until the whole of Jerusalem is conquered and reclaimed for him and the name of 'Israel' expunged from the map.

It has therefore become impossible to separate Western Islam from the Middle East crisis in our thinking. The crisis there is bound to affect Muslims everywhere. It will have a negative influence on their assimilation into Western society.

Though it is undoubtedly true that there are many peace-loving, law-abiding, hard-working, freedom-enjoying Muslims living in the West, it has to be said that this is at the cost of being less than true to their own religion. To put it bluntly, can they be sufficiently corrupted to be fully assimilated to our relativistic pluralism or will they, when faced with an ultimate choice, favour the faith of their fathers above patriotism to their adopted countries?

All this assumes that they have a free choice either to adhere rigidly to the principles and practice of Islam or to adapt both to fit into the prevailing culture. We must also ask about Islam itself. Do they hold it or does it hold them? Apart from sanctions against apostates, is there a power within or behind Islam that grips its followers over and above their own will? Are we dealing with supernatural as well as natural factors as we speculate about possible trends? The answer lies in an examination of the source from which it sprang.

6

Its Source

All religion comes from somewhere. Each expression of it has a geographical and historical beginning, which we have already looked at in the case of Islam (in Chapter 1). In this chapter we are probing deeper than space and time origin, seeking to identify its spiritual source. From where does it derive its spiritual inspiration and authority?

As with all religious phenomena, there are three possible answers. The first is a 'natural' explanation, increasingly popular in an age of scientific humanism and relativism. In brief, religion is a human invention, the product of our imagination and the result of our reaction to the universe in which we live. The forces of 'nature' are so much greater than our puny powers that we personalise them into 'gods' and seek to manipulate them for our benefit by devising ways to propitiate them. Such rationalisation is bound to decline as science removes mystery from the behaviour of our environment and gives us increasing mastery over it, animism being the first victim.

The alternative is a 'supernatural' explanation, that there are powers, personal powers, above and beyond the natural universe and therefore beyond the reach of scientific investigation. Knowledge of these can be obtained only if they choose to reveal themselves to us in a way we can comprehend. Judaism, Christianity and Islam all claim to have received such a revelation and recorded it in what then becomes their sacred scripture.

However, there is a further complication. All three religions believe in supernatural, or at least superhuman, beings who are under God's ultimate control but given a degree of free will, as we are. Some are good (angels, led by archangels) and some are bad (demons, led by the devil). They have greater power and intelligence than ourselves and can have a temporary but terrible influence on human affairs.

There are therefore virtually three possible sources of any world religion: divine inspiration, human imagination or satanic imitation. From which of these has Islam sprung? A case can be made out for any one of these or a mixture of two but certainly not all three, since God and Satan are hardly likely to have co-operated in any production!

DIVINE INSPIRATION?

Every Muslim is convinced that the Quran, on which Islam is based, was a revelation from Allah, the one and only God, to Muhammad, his messenger. Furthermore, it was a word-for-word dictated version of a document already written in heaven. As each part was received, over three decades, the prophet remembered and recited it to his followers, who wrote it down on any available material. Later, these were collected and issued in an authorised compendium, believed to be the final, definitive and infallible Word of God.

There are some variations in the Quran itself as to exactly how it came to Muhammad, from Allah appearing as a man, to an angel, Gabriel, speaking on his behalf. The latter is the most widely accepted. And there was some variation between early collections of Muhammad's 'recitations', but others were destroyed when the official version was sanctioned.

Since it was given in the Arabic language, it must be kept and read in that. Translations into other languages are mere paraphrases and not to be regarded as the Quran. Only the original text is divinely inspired and God's final word to mankind, correcting and completing all other previous revelations through his prophets.

That, then, is the claim at the heart of Islam. On what grounds is it accepted by so many? Actually, very little evidence is offered to substantiate it. Muslim apologists point to its beautiful prose and poetry, which could not have originated from a self-confessed illiterate. Others simply say it could not have so successfully convinced so many in so many cultures and countries unless God was behind it.

But in practice it is largely accepted as a leap of faith rather than a step of reason. Islam is self-authenticating in a circular kind of way. The Quran says Muhammad is the prophet of God and he says it is the Word of God. Each validates the other, so one either believes both or neither. There is a noticeable absence of independent corroboration or objective evidence. There is very little content in the Quran that can be examined in the light of external criteria.

However, there is one reason for seriously questioning this claim. The existence of the Quran is a fact to be faced, but so is the existence of the Bible, which also makes a similar claim to be God's full and final revelation, not just of his will for us but of his very self.

One thing is crystal clear. The Bible and the Quran cannot possibly both be the Word of God. So many are the contradictions between them that a choice has to be made.

Of course, they could both be wrong, neither being God's revelation. But they cannot both be right, genuine revelations of the same God. To recognise one is to reject the other.

Some of the numerous contradictions are relatively minor disagreements over historical detail. The Quran says God created the world in eight days; one of Noah's sons refused to go into the Ark and was drowned; Abraham lived in Mecca, rebuilt the *Ka'aba* built by Adam, had only two sons, not eight, was willing to sacrifice Ishmael not Isaac; Moses was adopted by Pharaoh's wife, witnessed Noah's flood, saw crucifixions, etc. That last point is one of many anachronisms: Nimrod and Abraham were contemporaries, as were Haman and Moses; Mary the Mother of Jesus was the sister of Moses and Aaron (Miriam is Hebrew for Mary).

Far, far more serious are the contradictions about Jesus. The Quran accepts his virgin birth (i.e. conception), but denies his pre-existence; accepts his miraculous powers and sinless character, but rejects his claim to be the unique Son of God; denies his crucifixion and therefore his resurrection also, but accepts his ascension and future return. Above all, Isa, as they call him, was only an apostle of God, prior to and inferior to Muhammad.

Above all, there is a fundamental contradiction about the nature of God himself, whether one solitary person or three persons in one. While the word 'Trinity' is not in the New Testament, the facts of which it is a shorthand summary certainly are (including the application of 'God' to the man Jesus). Even allowing for Muhammad's mistaken notion that the 'three' were Father, Mother and Jesus (probably picked up from Syrian churches who called Mary 'Mother of God' and hung pictures of her alongside those of Jesus), his words nevertheless condemned all plurality in God as blasphemous polytheism. More of that later.

To sum up and highlight the major gulf between the Quran and the Bible, one need only quote the angel Gabriel in both. He told Mary that her son would be called the Son of God (Luke 1:32) but said to Muhammad: 'Far be it from his (Allah's) glory that he should have a son.' Gabriel could have said either but surely not both.

Muslims are fully aware of these obvious contradictions. So to the claim for the truthfulness of their own scriptures they add the charge that Jews and Christians have corrupted theirs to include lies. They offer no evidence as to who was responsible or when and how the fraud was perpetrated. The early manuscripts of the New Testament demonstrate the falsity of this accusation.

We shall look later at the considerable evidence underscoring the reliability of the Jewish and Christian scriptures contained in the Bible. What we are pointing out here is that for Christians who believe the Bible to contain the true revelation of God, they have to deny the divine inspiration of Muhammad and the Quran and look at the other two possible sources.

HUMAN IMAGINATION?

Muslims are offended when their religion is called: 'Muhammadanism'. Like some Christian labels (Lutheranism, Calvinism, Wesleyanism), it implies following the teaching of a man. Muhammad is not believed to have had any personal influence on the content of the Quran. As a 'messenger' he simply repeated what had been dictated to him.

Nevertheless, a case can be made for some human input, whether conscious or sub-conscious. There is the fact that the revelations were in the Arabic language, even with traces of the dialect of Mecca. There is the use of other sources, which could have been picked up in travels. Some are Arabic legends – the she-camel becoming a prophet; seven men and their animals sleeping in a cave for 309 years. Some are from the fraudulent 'Gnostic' Gospels – Jesus speaking as a baby, making clay birds come alive as a boy. Some are from Sabean rituals – praying five times a day, fasting for part of a day over one month. Some are from Zoroastrianism and Hinduism.

There are the 'mistakes' when quoting Bible history (we have already noted some contradictions). But these are understandable since the Jewish and Christian scriptures had not been translated into Arabic and Muhammad could not have read them anyway. His misunderstanding of the Trinity as Father, Mother Mary and Son Jesus is explained by what he saw rather than what he heard in Christian worship.

There are discernible changes in teaching from the earlier suras (which are shorter and towards the end of the Quran) to the later (which are longer and come earlier). For example, the shift from praying towards Jerusalem to praying towards Mecca and from Saturday 'sabbath' to Friday, changes which correspond to a deteriorating relationship with the Jewish people.

There are personal concessions to himself, allowing Muhammad to have more than four wives, the limit for all other Muslims, or to take his adopted son's wife as his own, after due divorce.

There are dozens of indications of human authorship and, indeed, fallibility. It is, nevertheless, a remarkable and impressive compilation. If the source of the Quran is human, then it is the work of a genius, who by it was able to turn a whole nation from polytheistic idolatry to monotheistic simplicity and in the process bring warring tribes into peaceful unity. All that is no mean achievement and at the least shows Muhammad to be an outstanding man, not to be under-estimated for his influence on human history.

Some Christians, while believing their Bible to be the true Word of God, nevertheless find some divine inspiration in the Quran, as well as human imagination. They see it as a mixture of sources containing truth and error. Their criterion for judging which is which is simple. Where it agrees with the Bible, it delivers truth from God and where it disagrees we have unreliable human speculation. Some of those taking this view would attribute the true parts to 'general revelation', that indirect and instinctive awareness of God available to the whole human race, but others would claim that to Muhammad was given a measure of direct 'special revelation'. Either way, they would base their assessment on the similarities between the Bible and the Quran, while playing down the differences, motivated by a desire to establish common ground between Christians and Muslims as a pre-evangelistic strategy. They emphasise that both teach 'God as Creator and Judge', the all-merciful and compassionate 'One'. That the two scriptures have some, even much, truth in common is undeniable but we must never overlook the many and deep disagreements.

There is, however, another explanation for the 'truth' in the Quran, which Christians must consider.

SATANIC IMITATION

This possibility comes to mind when the 'natural' explanation appears inadequate. The amazing hold (I nearly wrote 'stranglehold') Islam has on over a billion people today, to say nothing of millions of others over the last fourteen centuries, points to more power and authority than could be exercised by a single individual who died so long ago. It is not hard to see an 'unearthly' force behind it.

There is the unusual physical state in which Muhammad received his revelations, not unlike a trance or a seizure. When this first happened, he thought the evil spirits (jinn or genies) were taking possession of him, but his older wife convinced him it was from God.

We know that behind pagan worship of idols are demons (1 Corinthians 10:20). While Muhammad destroyed all 360 idols in Mecca, he kept some things associated with them, such as the *Ka'aba* (Cube) building, with its sacred black stone, probably a meteorite, and still revered. The name 'Allah' came out of this pantheon and his father's name, Abdullah (servant of Allah) confirms this. At one stage he seemed to make a concession to the polytheism of Mecca by including a revelation about three daughters of the male moon-god and the female sun-god, two of whom bore names compounded from 'Allah'. He later repented of this, acknowledged that the devil (Shaitan) had deceived him and this was excluded from the final collection (these were the 'satanic verses' to which the writer Salman Rushdie drew attention, attracting a sentence of death, a fatwah, for his blasphemy).

But none of this would justify a demonic explanation. However, there are three features of the whole that could indicate it, summed up in three words: deception, distraction and destruction.

Deception The devil is a master of disguise, rarely if ever appearing as he actually is. The naive caricature of a being with horns and a forked tail, dressed from head to foot in black, is complete speculation. If he ever came like that he would be readily recognised and rebuffed! He came to Adam and Eve in the guise of an animal (a lizard with legs, not a snake yet). He addressed Jesus through one of his best friends, Peter (Matthew 16:23). Paul assumed that 'Satan himself masquerades as an angel of light' (2 Corinthians 11:14). He could easily mimic the angel Gabriel.

However, his major method of deception is to mix truth with error. Outright lies can easily be spotted, though even they can be believed. But it is the half-truth that is particularly dangerous, precisely because there is truth in it. But it is never the whole truth and nothing but the truth. From the beginning, in the garden of Eden, the devil has cleverly mixed truth and error in just the right proportions to confuse and control his victims (Genesis 3:4–5). Even when tempting Jesus, he quoted the words of God in scripture (Matthew 4:6), usually out of context. The devil knows the truth, from his original location with God in heaven, and being far more intelligent than any human being can manipulate it for his own ends.

This could explain the mixture of affirmation and denial of truth in the Quran. God is one but not three. Jesus is human but not divine. He was born of a virgin but did not die on a cross. He did many miracles but was not raised from the dead. The Bible is revelation but not reliable. Jews and Christians are 'People of the Book' but not the people of God.

The practical effect of all this brings us to the second characteristic of the devil's devices.

Distraction He skilfully draws attention away from vital truths, often without his victims being aware of it. Again we see it from the first encounter with Eve. With a subtle exaggeration of what God had said, he caused Eve's gaze to focus on what God had forbidden and notice its attraction, to divert her from the many trees whose fruit God had given her to enjoy to the only one she was forbidden.

Islam has succeeded only too well in diverting interest from the God of the Bible to the Allah of the Quran, from Jesus to Muhammad and above all, from salvation through faith to salvation by works. The overall impression is that Islam has superseded Christianity and its predecessor Judaism, rendering both obsolete. It appears as a brilliant diversionary tactic. But it is also a destructive one.

Destruction The devil is unable to create from nothing, as God has done. His resentment boils over in taking a delight in destroying what God has created. One of his titles is 'the Destroyer'.

We have noted above the subtle undermining of Biblical religion by implying its obsolescence. But Islam has a more direct destructive aspect than that. From the lifetime of Muhammad on, Jews and Christians have been killed in the name of Allah. Now, in the twenty-first century, the majority of Christian martyrdoms take place in Muslim countries such as Indonesia, Sudan and Nigeria. Western civilisation, identified by many Muslims as 'Christian' in name if not in nature, is hated and despised.

The fact is that violence and terrorism are often associated with Islamic countries and groups. The Quran *can* be understood as encouraging martyrdom and even murder. Indeed, those who commit atrocities may be taking their faith more seriously than fellow Muslims who want to live in Western society and are therefore anxious to promote an image of a peaceable, non-aggressive version of their religion. Quite simply, Muslims expect all other faiths to disappear eventually and give place to their own. However this is achieved, whether by evolution or revolution, this spells the death-knell of the Judeo-Christian faith of the Bible.

We have looked at the three possible sources from which Islam and its basic scripture, the Quran, could have sprung. We have pointed out that the Christian who believes the Bible to be the true Word of God is driven to consider one or both of the other possibilities. Readers who have come to share the conclusion that there is a supernatural power other than God behind it must consider some very important implications of this diagnosis.

The first is that Muslims are not our enemies. Nor is Islam itself to be regarded as an adversary. A first requirement in any conflict is an accurate identification of opposing forces and assessment of their capability. In this case, Christians need Paul's reminder that 'our struggle is not against flesh and blood, but against the rulers, against the authorities, against the power of this dark world and against the spiritual forces of evil in the heavenly realms' (Ephesians 6:12).

The second is that since these rulers, authorities and powers are spiritual and not physical, 'carnal' warfare is worse than useless against them. Military Crusades in the past have done more harm than good to the Christian cause. To bring this up to date, attempts to block the building of mosques in this country through local legislative bodies should not be engaged in, unless existing bye-laws to protect the community's welfare are being blatantly overridden. For similar reasons, it is hypocrisy to oppose the extension of blasphemy laws to cover Islam while wanting to keep them in place for Christianity. Better to abolish them altogether and treat blasphemy as a sin against God rather than a crime against society. For Christians to use political power to impose the values and standards of their faith on unbelievers is to come dangerously near to what we have described as the 'essence' of Islam, the establishment of a theocracy. Christ has not commissioned Christians to do that.

The third is that Muslims need to be liberated from the bondage their religion could be exposing them to. Jesus came to set captives at liberty, demonstrated this by casting out demons, showing compassion for those thus oppressed and proclaiming the truth that would set us all free from the chains that bound us all to self, sin and Satan. Muslims need this deliverance as much as Christians formerly did. God is in the business of dispensing undeserved grace to his enemies (Romans 5:8–10). Christians are called to reflect this magnanimity in the face of any hostility towards them (Matthew 5:44–8; Romans 12:14–21).

We are already touching on the Christian response to the challenge of Islam, which will occupy our whole attention in the second section of this book.

Part Two

The Christian Response

7

Revelation?

My private premonition about an Islamic takeover of Britain is now a public prediction, prompting a debate about whether it is a 'prophecy' (a divine revelation) or not. Where did it come from?

One thing is quite clear. No-one else said it to me. I must take full responsibility for saying it – and blame, if necessary. So did the thought originate in my mind?

Not consciously, since it was not the result of any analytical examination of current trends or prolonged meditation. It came right out of the blue, as much a surprise to me as to others. Some have said they share my concern but disagree with my 'conclusion'. But it was never a conclusion drawn from evidence for me. It was the beginning and foundation of my later investigation.

What about my subconscious? The Assistant Secretary of the Baptist Union claimed I was suffering an identity crisis, presumably hinting that I needed to make a sensational statement to recover a role in the public eye. She cannot have been aware of the worldwide distribution of my tapes, books and videos, together with radio and television broadcasts. I have neither the need nor the desire for publicity. Others have postulated a pathological pessimism, amounting to a death wish, or a perverted ambition to be provocatively controversial. I do have a desire to make people think for themselves and re-examine cherished traditions but I don't relish the suspicion and isolation that sometimes results.

So if neither others nor myself are the origin, we are left with either a demonic or divine influence. We know that Satan is the Destroyer, particularly of human relationships with each other and their Maker, deepening rifts whenever he can. But he is an enemy of truth as well as unity and, as we have seen, a master of deception. I can only say that I have submitted my message to Christian leaders gifted with discernment and not one has even suspected satanic influence. At worst, I have been accused of mistaken thinking.

So why do I think I received a prophetic prediction from the Lord? A minor reason is that it was not only totally unexpected but also deeply unwelcome. It was bad, not good news. I thought of my children and grandchildren living with this. Indeed, I was so reluctant to accept it that in the recorded version I freely admitted, 'I hope I am wrong; I hope it is a false prophecy.' But that was my 'flesh' speaking, not my 'spirit'.

A positive reason was that it came to me in the same way and with the same force as other insights into the future, some of which had considerable political significance and were later proved to be accurate and inspired by the Lord. One was that Margaret Thatcher would become British Prime Minister. I was therefore the first person to congratulate her (well before the election) and passed on to her two things the Lord wanted her to give priority to. She mentioned one in her first press interview as she entered 10 Downing Street and declared her intention of fulfilling it – and did the other within her first month. Lest any reader conclude that God is a Tory, right-wing in his thinking, let me add that in the same way I announced in Australian churches that a trade union leader, Bob Hawke, was God's next choice for their Prime Minister. To cries of: 'How dare you mention that boozing womaniser in church?' I replied: 'Scripture commands us to pray for those in authority and if you start now he may turn out much better than you think', which he did. I have learned to trust my spirit when such unexpected promptings come, but I would be the last to claim to get it right every time.

Of course, the ultimate test of any prophetic prediction is whether it comes true. Moses made this plain when he warned Israel not to be afraid of prophets who speak presumptuously and whose forecasts are not fulfilled (Deuteronomy 18:21–2, a text that makes me afraid of myself!). But the test of time is somewhat unhelpful. By the time an event does or does not occur, it is normally too late to do anything about it, which was the point of the prediction in the first place!

There is a more immediate test available. Prophecies are to be 'weighed and judged' (affirmed or denied) 'by others', not the prophets themselves. For this reason, I submitted my message to Christian leaders around the country over a period of weeks. I did not always present it as a 'prophecy', but often as a 'conviction', bearing in mind two extreme reactions to the former. On the one hand, many Christians do not believe that God gives prophecies today, but only 'speaks' through the completed canon of scripture. On the other, other Christians are reluctant to question anyone who claims 'Thus saith the Lord', for fear of sinning against the Holy Spirit.

As might be expected, I got a wide variety of response to my announcement of an Islamic takeover, ranging over the whole spectrum of – unimaginable, impossible, improbable, possible, probable, unavoidable. Many said it *could* happen; these ranged from unlikely to likely. But a surprising number agreed it *would* happen, having already come to that conclusion before I mentioned it (one said he came to it twenty years previously). However, none of these had shared this sombre certainty on a public platform and it was this group that urged me to speak out.

I tried to be as objective as I could, aware of the subtle temptation to focus on sympathetic or supportive comments. I paid particular attention to those most acquainted with contemporary prophecy, but even here there were mixed signals. Dr Clifford Hill, founder of Prophetic Word Ministries and the magazine *Prophecy Today*, circulated a special tape 'to protect the body of Christ from this false prophecy', though he had 'deliberately not listened to my message lest his judgement be unduly influenced'. At a subsequent conference his colleague David Noakes, who had listened to my message, gave a word in which he twice promised, in the name of the Lord, that this country would never be allowed to fall into the hands of Islam. Both, however, have subsequently issued a statement, including: 'There is strong evidence that God is using Islam as the "rod of his anger" against the church because of our apostasy.' More recently, Dr Hill has written in his magazine: 'If we fail to respond rightly [to the "threat" of Islam to our Christian heritage] Britain will become an Islamic nation in one or two generations at the most.' So we may not be so far apart after all.

One consultant I have already quoted was Joel Edwards, who directs the Evangelical Alliance. I sought his opinion because of his wide contacts in church and nation. We had met unexpectedly at the induction of Greg Haslam to the pastorate of Westminster Chapel so I took the opportunity to ask him if I could 'run something past him'. On getting his consent I made the categorical statement: 'I believe this country will become Islamic.' After a sharp intake of breath, which he vividly recalls, he simply said: 'You're right.' It was now my turn to be taken aback, having expected anything from an outright denial to a qualified comment, but not an immediate endorsement. However, he subsequently issued a statement on his web-site, containing two qualifications. One, that he had not meant his comment 'for the public domain'. He had not indicated this to me in any way ('in confidence', 'between ourselves' or 'off the record' would have done) but I take this opportunity to apologise if he feels I betrayed a confidence. Two, that he had meant that it *could* happen but not necessarily *would* happen. But he went on to add such compelling reasons why it could happen that many, including *Christianity and Renewal* magazine assumed he was 'concurring with my conclusion' (that word again!).

Anglican response was noticeably muted. Advertising tapes in the 'low' *Church of England Newspaper* and the 'high' *Church Times* brought little or no requests, whereas other Christian publications brought many. Two groups welcomed my contribution – non-Muslim Christians working for and among Muslims, and ex-Muslims who had become Christians.

Surprising confirmation came from outside Christian circles. A leading Muslim citizen of Leicester, Sulyman Nagdi, JP, MBE, commenting on my prediction, reassuringly (?) said: 'We are the second largest religion in England, yes. But I think we have a long time to go before this (i.e. a takeover of the nation) happens. It isn't something that is going to happen in the next five or ten years.' So we have a breathing space even if he thinks it inevitable! The Professor of Islamic History in the Hebrew University of Jerusalem, Moshe Sharon, told me he believes Britain will be the first Western nation to succumb to Islam as it seeks expansion into Europe.

Some Christians commented that they would have preferred that my message had been given without this prediction, since they could give whole-hearted approval to all the rest. To them it raised unnecessary controversy, which could prevent the whole from reaching many. Actually, without it I would never have prepared the message for recording or printing and without the prediction it is very doubtful whether much notice would have been taken, though I did not include it for that reason. It added an urgent dimension on the back of which the whole message has gained attention.

As well as comments came questions, two in particular, about what I believed the Lord had shown me. Is it *immediate*? How soon could we expect it to happen? I had been careful to avoid any dating, since I had received no intimation whatsoever. One naughty Christian paper, *Evangelicals Now*, reported my message under the headline: 'Within a decade', which I had never said, and only stimulated scepticism. What I am sure of is that if the Lord is *telling* us now, then *now* is the time to start thinking about and preparing for this eventuality.

Is it *inevitable*? Again, I was careful to avoid this word, since God has free will and can change his mind about what he intends to do, even in response to human pleading. Moses and Amos spring to mind. But the clearest example in scripture is that of Jonah, whose unconditional and dated announcement of the destruction of Nineveh never happened because its entire population repented, and God took pity on the innocent children and dumb animals who would have been caught up in the disaster. In fact, Jonah himself suspected that God would let them off and therefore let him down as a prophet, which was why he had fled to Tarshish in the first place (Jonah 4:1–3; cf. 2 Kings 14:23–7). But he was as much concerned about the Lord's reputation as his own, convinced that the Ninevites would not take his anger seriously and would return to their wicked ways. Jonah was right and they did. A century and a half later God sent Nahum to say that divine patience was exhausted, their condition incurable and their destruction absolutely certain (Nahum 3:19). Just as Jonah was obedient in delivering the unconditional warning, I felt I had to do the same, with no 'if' or 'unless' about it, just as I received it, while God in his sovereignty is perfectly at liberty to change his tactics, but not his ultimate purposes. Is he likely to do so in this case?

As an evangelical I like to have scriptural backing for what I preach and teach. But there is no mention of Islam in the Bible or of its growth to be a worldwide religion, much less of its takeover of Britain. In the absence of any direct reference, I asked the Lord if there was any analogous situation, which would throw a light on what he was doing here and now. Again and again my thoughts were drawn to another 'minor prophet', not Jonah but Habakkuk. During my long preaching ministry I had frequently told my congregation about this man who dared to argue with God. He did not win the argument (who could?) but he did get clear answers to his complaints.

Deeply concerned about the moral and spiritual decline in Israel, he accused the Lord of indifference, of doing nothing about the dire situation. The Lord replied that he was already tackling the problem by bringing an invading force from Babylon (modern Iraq) to deal with it. Habakkuk immediately swung to the opposite extreme and complained that God was doing too much rather than too little! Aware of the Babylonian 'scorched earth' policy, wiping out all plant, animal and human life, the prophet pointed out that the remedy was far too drastic. Even if Jerusalem deserved such a fate, God would be left without any of his chosen people to worship and represent him. Habakkuk even tried to tie God down with his own character by arguing that his eyes were too pure to watch such a wicked slaughter of all his people. God's answer was clear and simple: 'The just (who live righteously) shall live (survive the holocaust) by faith (remaining faithful to me).' Even in the New Testament this text, when quoted, emphasises the need for *continuity* of trusting the Lord, whatever happens (Romans 1:17; Hebrews 10:38–9), in order to come safely through times of judgement.

This promise assured Habakkuk that the coming trials were redemptive rather than retributive, a refining rather than a rejecting of his people, a hope rather than a threat. God was behind the Babylonians and knew exactly what he was doing with them for the benefit of his own. Habakkuk's emotions took another somersault and we find him singing and dancing for joy. The prospect had not changed but his perspective on it had. He was now convinced he would go on 'rejoicing in God my Saviour' even when the land was desolated. (I suggest that at this point the reader looks at the Appendix, which contains my poetic version of Habakkuk's triumphant song, as well as details of my recorded talks about his message.)

Habakkuk was told to announce the divine intention as publicly as possible, putting it on hoardings in the street, so that 'he who runs (past) may read' and 'he who reads may run (to tell others)'. The Hebrew may be translated either way! In my own small way I felt constrained to do the same, using the greater variety of media available today. Like him, I felt the need to tell anybody who will listen, look or read not only *what* was coming but *why* it was coming.

For my 'revelation' did not stop with the prediction of an Islamic takeover of Britain. Indeed, one of the main reasons why I came to believe its roots were in divine inspiration rather than human intuition was that further thoughts 'came' to me which had the same stamp of insight and authority.

Over the years I have developed what I call 'interrogatory' prayer (asking God questions), as distinct from 'intercessory' prayer (asking God for favours). Learning to wait for answers and recognise his voice has been part of it, but from time to time answers have clearly come, though I would be the last to claim a hotline to heaven. They have usually been crystal clear but 'telegraphic', just a word or a few words, rarely more than a sentence or two.

My first question in this case was: 'Why are you telling me (about this future development)?' A single sentence was as clearly in my mind as if I had just read or heard it: 'Because my Church is unaware and unready.' That naturally led on to: 'In what way? How can we get ready?' to which the unexpected response was simply three words, all beginning with the letter 'R': 'Reality. Relationship. Righteousness.' And that was all.

— Those familiar with my preaching will know that I am given to alliteration. It is said to be 'the province of fools, poets and Plymouth Brethren'! But it is an aid to memory (who, having heard a phrase like 'short sharp shock' will have any difficulty with instant recall?), mainly because poetry stays in the memory far more readily than prose. At first I suspected my own thinking was affecting what I was hearing. Then I wondered if God was pandering to my weakness. Finally, I remembered that most biblical prophecies were given in poetic form for good reasons and that the Lord wanted these words to be planted deeply in our minds. I call them 'the three R's' (formerly associated with 'reading, 'riting and 'rithmetic'!).

I meditated on them for months and the fruits of that are found in the next three chapters. I believe them to constitute the divine diagnosis of the basic deficiencies that leave us vulnerable to attack. One of the uncertainties that my prediction has aroused is whether the Church will survive. The answer is positive if these three basic needs are addressed, negative if they are ignored.

Readers who have studied the page of contents will have already noticed that there are six chapters in this second 'Christian' section in this book, all beginning with the letter 'R'. Only three of these 'came' to me, I believe from the Lord. Nor am I trying to add to this. The other three (the present chapter and the final two) come from me. I have added a question mark to their titles to distinguish them. Why are they included?

As might be expected, there has been much debate and dialogue since the recorded message was released (at the end of August 2002) and circulated so widely. Discussion has focused on its possible cause and effect. I have had to think a great deal about these practical aspects and am now in a position to say more about them. I have dealt with the past aspect in this chapter and will deal with the future, both immediate and ultimate outcomes, in Chapters 11 and 12.

In all three my remarks are more tentative and presented for consideration. They represent my response to what has been said to (and about!) me. I claim no more for them than that and hope they will be discussed in the same spirit with which they are offered. The question mark in their titles is an invitation to do just that, as well as a recognition that under these heads there may well be genuine differences among sincere and even evangelical Christians.

But Chapters 8, 9 and 10 are quite different. I present them with a confidence which some may find is too dogmatic. But I believe that their main thrust is not up for debate. The reader's choice is between reception or rejection, depending on whether the stamp of God's truth is discerned or not. I am content to let others judge.

8

Reality

'All the religions in the world could be wrong but only one can be right!' These were the words with which I began to address a grammar school assembly of 850 boys, having been pressed to respond to a buzz of interest in Islam, following the visit of a Muslim speaker. I spent the rest of my talk focusing on the 'real' issues and received a spontaneous ovation.

The real question is, to quote Pontius Pilate: 'What is truth?' 'Truth' and 'reality' are synonyms in any English thesaurus, but they are also the very same word in the biblical languages of Hebrew and Greek and may be interchangeably translated. When Paul talked about 'the only true God', he meant: 'the only real God, the only God who really exists'. The answer to Pilate's question was standing a few feet in front of him, for Jesus claimed to be '*The* truth'. He was not just saying: 'I'm for real,' but: 'I'm the Reality behind all other realities,' the kind of statement that forces you to decide whether he was mad, bad or God!

'Truth' has other synonyms, such as 'actuality', 'accuracy', 'authenticity', all of which highlight the vital issue of discerning which claims to truth correspond to the real facts of our existence. It does matter whether our universe is the result of chance or choice, whether there is a God or not and whether we are responsible to him or simply to ourselves and each other.

➤ The search for truth is hindered by our preference for fantasy rather than fact, illustrated by our leisure pursuits when we can choose our interests and activities as over against our daily work in the 'real' world. Books and films such as *Lord of the Flies* and *Lord of the Rings* are greater attractions than anything about the Lord of the universe. Attention has shifted from objective reality 'out there' to subjective reality 'in here'. But 'true' religion must be primarily concerned with the former rather than the latter.

However meaningful and supportive any religious faith may be to its adherents, we must still insist that this is no more than a placebo unless its tenets correspond to the realities of life in the universe and are in that sense 'scientific'. Otherwise we are living in delusion, which is ultimately self-deceptive and self-destructive. We need to find the truth that is as true for everybody as for anybody, and the truth that remains true whether it is believed by anybody or nobody.

It does not necessarily make much difference whether we believe in a divine being called 'God' or not. Far more significant is the question: 'What *kind* of God do you (or do you not) believe in?' It has been said that we should never condemn an atheist until we have found out what kind of God he was told to believe in! When we ask this, we soon discover how radically different the major religions are from each other, the mutual contradictions preventing all but the naïve and ignorant from thinking of them as basically the same. It will help to see this if we ask two subsidiary questions.

Person or Thing? Is 'God' simply a higher power or cosmic force to which we can be attuned, or does 'God' possess a heart, mind and will, the ingredients of personality, to whom we can relate? Is 'God' a he (or a she?) or an it? Buddhism gives one answer and Islam another. And there is a world of difference between 'God bless you' and 'may the force be with you'.

One or Many? After centuries of Christian influence, we have become so used to using the word 'God' in the singular that it seems strange that others could believe in a multitude of gods (and goddesses). Hinduism claims there have been many such 'divine manifestations', up to 30 million say some. Islam is horrified by the thought and emphatically insists on the 'oneness' of Allah.

THE ONE GOD

These contradictions are obvious but it is a different matter when the three 'monotheistic' religions are compared. It is all too easily assumed that they are all worshipping one and the same God under different names – 'Yahweh' for the Jew (though it is rarely spoken, for fear of taking it in vain, and is substituted by euphemisms like 'heaven'; even 'God' is never fully spelled in print, but only 'G-d'); 'Father' for the Christian; and 'Allah' for the Muslim. Or perhaps such different names point to three different gods? The position is much more complicated than that.

For one thing, Christians are convinced that their God is one and the same as the God of Israel, hence the inclusion of the Jewish scriptures, the 'Old Testament', in the Christian Bible. 'Yahweh' was not only Jesus' God as a practising Jew but also his Father in a unique way. Christians believe they know more about this God than Jews but nothing which contradicts what they already knew.

However, the Church, which quickly adopted an anti-Semitic attitude to its Jewish roots, abandoned the Hebrew name that God had revealed to Israel. Either the word 'LORD' (in capital letters in English translations of the Bible) was used instead, or the four letters 'JHVH' (pronounced 'Yahweh') were given English pronunciation with added phonetic vowels: 'Jehovah'), now rarely used. A recent and excellent Roman Catholic version, the *Jerusalem Bible*, has restored the Hebrew name 'Yahweh'.

There is even more confusion in translations of the Bible into Arabic, where 'God' is invariably rendered 'Allah', justifying this by claiming that it is simply the Arab word for 'God'. But that is not so. A literal translation of the Islamic creed is: 'There is no god but The-God'. The first 'god' is simply a generic or general description (like 'sea') but the second use of the word, integrated with the definite article, making it exclusive (equivalent to 'the *only* God'), has become a specific title and virtually become a name (like 'Atlantic' or 'Pacific'). The battle-cry of Arab warriors, *Allah akbar* ('God is great') is clearly this usage.

In Jewish scriptures *Elohim* is the 'generic' word for God (significantly a plural form for at least three 'gods', though the verbs attached are always singular), and 'Yahweh' is the specific name, used over 9,000 times, while 'Allah' is not used once. The complete reverse is the case in the Quran.

THE TRINITARIAN GOD

But the difference between the God of the Muslims and the God of Christians is far from being only a matter of name. There is a radical difference, amounting to an irreconcilable difference in their natures as well as their names. It can be summed up in one word: 'Trinity'.

This word and what it represents are anathema to good Muslims, who abhor what they regard as polytheism (many gods), including tritheism (three gods). Mind you, Muhammad misunderstood the Christian 'three' as a 'family' of God the Father, Jesus (Arabic *Isa*) the Son, and Mary the Mother (some Christians may have been responsible for giving this impression). And it has been further assumed that Christians believe the Father had carnal relations with the Mother to produce the Son. But even when these caricatures have been corrected, the gulf remains, as more Muslims than Christians seem to realise. Granted that the word 'Trinity' is not found in the Bible and was coined much later (by a North African Christian called Tertullian), the experiences and convictions for which it is a shorthand summary are integral to the New Testament. Jews were as strictly and ardently monotheistic as later Muslims, believing in one person called God, in spite of a hint otherwise in their creed (the *Shema*, from Deuteronomy: 'Hear, O Israel, Yahweh our gods, Yahweh is one'). Yet when a Jew called Jesus (in Hebrew: *Yeshua*) was born, lived, died and came back to life among them, at first a dozen, then hundreds, then thousands became convinced that he was as fully divine as he was fully human and could be called 'Lord and God', as well as Yahweh, whom he called his 'Father'. That Father and Son were quite distinct persons was never in doubt. They talked about and to each other, as they also did about a third person, 'the Holy Spirit', whom those same monotheistic Jews also came to know personally, shortly after Jesus left the earthly scene.

Yet they never doubted for one moment that in meeting, knowing and loving all three distinct and divine persons they were still dealing with only one God. They never referred to the God they worshipped and served as 'they' or 'them', but only and always as 'he' or 'him'. The unity or 'oneness' of God was not to be found in singleness of personhood but in the perfect harmony of thought, feeling and intention shared between them and in their complementary functions in pursuing an identical purpose. That one of the three had become and continues to be a human being like us simply adds to the wonder. That the divine being stretches our intellect and imagination to their limits and beyond is hardly surprising. We would have to be gods ourselves to understand God fully.

The Trinity is the test and touchstone of genuine Christianity. From time to time, some Christians have overemphasised one person to the detriment of the other two (usually the Son, but sometimes the Spirit). And there have been sects claiming to be 'Christian' while denying the deity of Christ and the personality of the Spirit. The Unitarian churches of North America, Mormons and Jehovah's Witnesses are examples. But the Church as a whole has doggedly maintained the definition of a Christian as someone having a personal trust in and relationship with Father, Son and Holy Spirit.

There is nothing like this anywhere in Islam. Though ninety-nine names (including titles) are attributed to Allah, there are two conspicuous by their absence, which cannot be used by Muslims but which lie at the heart of Christian devotion.

God is *Father*. Fatherhood is integral to divine being. He

always was a Father and always will be, because he always had a Son and always will have. It is his very nature, not just his name. This is not an 'anthropomorphic' projection of our relationship on to him but the exact opposite. He is 'the Father, from whom all fatherhood in heaven and on earth derives its name' (Ephesians 3:14–15; the Greek word is *patria*, often mistranslated as 'family'). No wonder the most widely read account of a conversion from Islam to Christianity is entitled: *I Dared to Call Him Father*. And it is his only eternal Son who has made such a 'family' relationship possible. He calls those who believe in him his 'brothers' (Hebrews 2:11) and gives them the privilege of addressing his Father as 'our Father' (Matthew 6:9). Since this is all unique to himself, Jesus was perfectly in order to make the exclusive claim that: 'No-one comes to the Father except through me' (John 14:6). Without him none of this would have been possible. He plays such a unique role that scripture gives him over 250 names and titles, more than anyone else in history has ever held or deserved.

God is *Love*. At the same time the simplest and most profound statement, it could only have been made by a Christian, not even a Jew. It appears towards the end of the New Testament (1 John 4:8), because only after people were convinced that God was three persons in one could it be said. The fact is that one solitary person existing in isolation simply cannot *be* love. To put it another way, who did God love before he created anyone else he could love? To say 'himself' would be to accuse him of narcissism (named after a person called Narcissus in Greek myth who fell in love with his own reflection in a pool). But in God we find an outgoing rather than a self-centred love. The Father always loved the Son and the Spirit and they always loved him. When asked why God created the human race, I always reply: 'He already had one

son, whom he enjoyed so much he wanted a larger family.'
True love is inclusive rather than exclusive, desiring to extend
its reach, especially to those who lack and need it.

Imagine a Christianity stripped of the concept of a 'loving
Father'. Its heart will have been lost, though it may still have
something to say about the head and the will. God would still
be someone to obey, in the hope of avoiding hell or attaining
heaven, but hardly someone to 'love with all one's heart, mind,
soul and strength'. It would be a master-servant, not a father-
son relationship; a duty to endure, not a delight to enjoy.

It should be obvious by now that the difference between
the Muslim and the Christian concept of God is one of kind,
not of degree. Quite simply, Allah and the Father of Jesus are
not one and the same, as so many naïvely assume. The God
of the Bible and the God of the Quran are much too dissimilar
to be identified.

Why then, is there a resistance to such a clear conclusion
and a pressure to play down such manifest contradictions (the
most fundamental being the statement in the Quran that God
has no son, inscribed on the inside wall of the Dome of the
Rock in Jerusalem)? We shall consider some other reasons
later (in Chapter 11), but in a chapter entitled 'Reality', the
main one must be dealt with. If the Muslim and Christian
concepts are found to be incompatible, a further question
simply cannot be avoided:

Which is the 'true' God? Which God 'really' exists? Which
understanding of him corresponds to reality? A choice has to
be made. Not surprisingly, many are reluctant to choose,
because that involves controversy as well as commitment. To
believe one is to disbelieve the other. There is and can be no
such thing as a Christian Muslim or a Muslim Christian, as
both realise and acknowledge. Much easier to opt out of all
responsibility and cry: 'a plague on both your houses', or

take refuge in the comforting delusion that 'all (religious) roads lead to the same God'. This book is not written for such but for sincere seekers after truth who cannot be content with clichés.

But how can we know which God is the real one? Is there any objective evidence on which a verdict may be based or is it purely a matter of subjective preference, influenced by heredity and environment, a blind leap of faith one way or the other? Is it a matter of taste or truth? How does anyone decide?

THE BIBLICAL GOD

An overall comparison between the Quran and the Bible is a good place to begin. Both claim to be divine and definitive revelations from God, but which corresponds to realities we can check?

One obvious divergence is how little history there is in the Quran and how much there is in the Bible. The basic reason for that is a very different attitude to the importance of time. We have already noticed an apparent indifference to chronological accuracy in the Quran, springing from a lack of interest in the sequence of events. It represents words spoken and even written in heaven, above and outside time and only dictated in time by an angel. Hence the revelations are largely, though not entirely, unrelated to the historical process and contain more exhortations and admonitions than narrative.

By contrast the Bible is packed with stories, true stories. In fact, it is one big story from beginning to end, the story of our race and our universe. Why is so much of the Bible in narrative form, when compared with other sacred scriptures?

The answer goes to the heart of the Christian faith, which is only relevant in the present because it is rooted in the past and related to the future.

Time is significant for God, not because he is inside time but because time is inside him. He is not the detached, changeless, impassive, timeless God of Greek philosophy, but one who is directly involved with events in time and space, which is why the Hebrews called him the 'living' God, alive and active in our world, as well as dynamically interactive with the creatures to whom he has given life. Nietzsche's cliché 'God is dead' was not intended to deny his existence; simply his departure from this world to another, without denying his past activity here.

God is not so much the 'eternal Now', as even some Christians think and speak, but the God who was, is and is to come. It is a pity that modern English translations of the Bible seem to prefer 'eternal' to the older 'everlasting', which kept time and eternity together. My faith was disturbed when I studied theology at Cambridge under some professors who seemed to study scripture with a pair of scissors, cutting it up into pieces and discarding whatever did not 'fit' contemporary opinion. But my faith was restored even stronger by one book, *Christ and Time*, by a Swiss theologian, Oscar Cullmann. I realised the difference between the Hebrew notion of time as a line always moving forward, and the Greek notion of time as a circle, endlessly going back on itself. The Greeks saw God above and outside the circle; the Hebrews saw him on and in the line, working out his eternal purpose in temporal events. History *is* his story.

The Bible is a record of what our Almighty Maker has *done* in our world, supremely in his Son and always by his Spirit. That is why there is so much historical narrative in the Bible. It is also a record of what he has *said*, both directly (by moving air in audible and intelligible sounds; e.g. John 12:29) and indirectly (through many prophets). But most of his words are directly related to his deeds, predicting them before he acts, explaining and applying them afterwards.

So the Bible presents God as a real person with a real personality. He is a real person in heaven, and has been a real person on earth. And most of its information about him is taken from the 'real world' in which we live. The Bible is a book about real people in real places experiencing real events. It presents real history in real geography.

EXTERNAL EVIDENCE

All this gives the Bible a real advantage when assessed alongside other scriptures for its truthfulness. So much of it can be checked out, whether it is believed or not. The geography can be compared with any accurate atlas. The history can be subject to all the rules of historical investigation and evidence. For example, the combination of eyewitness testimony and circumstantial evidence for the resurrection of Jesus would be enough to convince any jury of the happening, which may explain why such a high proportion of professional lawyers are Christians (for more details see my *Explaining the Resurrection*, Sovereign World, 1993).

Archaeology has a role to play and in its early days was largely concentrated on biblical sites in the Middle East. Scores of fascinating books have been written but I recommend the reader to get hold of Professor David Rohl's recent books: *A Test of Time* and *Genesis: A Study in Civilisation*. His astonishing discoveries relating to Joseph's time in Egypt and even the Garden of Eden, a beautiful hidden valley still full of fruit trees, are all the more impressive since he is neither a Jew nor a Christian, with no vested interest in proving the Bible to be true, yet convinced that the Old Testament history is substantially accurate and trustworthy.

INTERNAL EVIDENCE

In a book like this, it is impossible to do more than hint at the huge amount of external evidence supporting the 'real truth' of the Bible. But there is an even more impressive piece of internal evidence, namely its predictions about the future. Nearly a quarter of its 'verses' contain such a prediction, especially concentrated in 'the prophets'. Some of its 66 books are little except these (Revelation springs to mind, with Daniel, Ezekiel and Zechariah not far behind). Scholars have largely agreed when they were spoken and written so we know they are genuine foretelling.

The statistics speak for themselves. There are over 700 (735 to be exact) separate and distinct predictions, some mentioned only once and one over 300 times (the return of Jesus to planet earth). Of these, nearly 600 (596 to be exact, or 81 per cent) have already been fulfilled, quite literally. Some are happening now, before our very eyes, like the second return of the Jewish people to the land promised to them 'for ever' by God (see Genesis 13:15 and Isaiah 11:11, quoted in his lengthy but little-known book: *The Chariots of Israel*, by Prime Minister Harold Wilson).

Not one prediction that could have been fulfilled by now has failed. The chances against this are astronomical. To take one example: Ezekiel prophesied that the city of Tyre would be stripped down to bare rock and thrown into the sea, a fate that has befallen no other city, before or since. Centuries later, Alexander the Great did just that, to build a causeway out to the offshore island whence the population had fled in all available boats on his impending arrival. I am told the statistical chance of this happening is one in 10^{39}!

The remaining 19 per cent are largely concerned with the end of the world as we know it, so it is hardly surprising if they have not been fulfilled – yet. It can be only ignorance or arrogance that causes people to look elsewhere for 'guestimates' about the future, from think-tanks to horoscopes (the latter are read daily by six out of ten men and seven out of ten women in the UK).

There remains the internal evidence (or problem, depending on which way they are viewed) of the miracles in the Bible, which we define as a natural event with a supernatural cause. These are scattered throughout its pages but bunched around key events in the story and key persons at the human end (Moses, Elijah, Jesus, Peter and Paul). The most significant for Jewish faith is the parting of the Red Sea and for the Christian the resurrection of Jesus.

The supernatural cause is beyond the reach of scientific investigation, so beyond scientific proof *or disproof.* Anyone who says that 'miracles are scientifically impossible' reveals that they have already taken a leap of faith into 'scientism', the belief that the 'natural' universe is all the reality there is or that it is a 'closed system' of cast-iron 'laws' impervious to any external control or intervention. Quantum physics has blown a large hole in this and shown us that the physical world is far more flexible and unpredictable than we had realised and at least made it more 'open' to possible supernatural intrusion.

Many try to 'explain away' the extraordinary miracles that permeate the Biblical narrative, either by denying their occurrence, though they can never prove it, or by resorting to coincidence, regarding them as a natural event happening by chance. It was 'good luck' that the eastern gale drove the shallow waters of the Reed Sea (as it should be called) just when the Hebrew slaves were escaping from Egypt and that the Jordan bank caved in, temporarily damming the river, just when they were entering Canaan.

Why should it seem so incredible that a God who created our physical world can also control it (the belief called 'theism')? Of course, one can choose to think that he created but cannot control it, as the maker of a clock can only then wind it up and let it run itself (the belief is called 'deism' and is quite common, even in churches).

But the miracles are still there, integral to the Biblical account of history, and their long-term effects, such as the survival of the nation born out of slavery in Egypt, are still with us. Supremely, the miracles performed by Jesus, on nature as well as people, are attested by contemporary accounts outside the Bible. John's Gospel calls them 'signs', pointing to who he really was. Some were so spectacular that only God himself could have had the necessary power and knowledge. Even if modern science can replicate a few on a small scale, it can only do so with technological equipment and financial resources that were simply not available 2,000 years ago – and none are accomplished by word of mouth alone.

There is a sharp contrast between Jesus and Muhammad. The Quran records no miracles by Muhammad, though those of Jesus are affirmed. Later Muslims clearly felt this reflected on the prophet they had come to venerate, and their traditions began to attribute such supernatural activity to him, even ascribing some miracles identical to those Jesus did.

We must conclude this chapter, already longer than intended. One conclusion is clear: that the Bible is the heart of the Christian claim to have found the 'one true (i.e. real)

God'. Muhammad called Christians and Jews, 'the People of the Book'. Without it, we would be as much in the dark about who God is and what he is like as anybody else, and would be left with only the clues in creation around us and conscience within us, though even these are enough to leave atheists and agnostics 'without excuse' (according to Paul in Romans 1:20).

Whether Christians will survive the growing encounter with Islam will largely depend on their confidence in their own scriptures. Tragically, this has been undermined from within Christian circles, especially by academic 'scholars'. So-called 'higher criticism' of the Bible began in Germany, but has spread to theological seminaries throughout the world. A trend began, which treated biblical narrative as myth and metaphor, stories containing spiritual, moral and even psychological 'truths', but not to be taken as having literally happened, more like the Icelandic sagas or Aesop's fables.

Of course, there is metaphorical fiction in the Bible, of which Jesus' parables are the best example, though their impact depends on the fact that they *could* have happened. And no-one takes every bit of the Bible literally, or we'd believe only animals will survive in an afterlife, sheep in heaven and goats in hell! The problem comes when the Biblical writers were clearly presenting historical events and these are 'mythologised' because the modern mind finds them difficult to believe. Once started along this path, it is difficult to stop. Adam and Eve were the first victims, soon joined by Noah, Jonah, and Abraham, Isaac and Jacob. Even Jesus himself was not immune. His virgin birth was the first to be doubted as having really happened, followed by his visible ascension into heaven and his future bodily return to earth. Above all, his physical resurrection, on which Christian faith and hope hang, must now be 'demythologised', as a story telling us how faith in him survived his death. An alarming number of bishops share this kind of sceptical speculation.

The authenticity and authority of Christianity rest on hard historical facts, not feelings, much less fantasy. Without such a foundation there would be very little on which to build a faith. Indeed, it is possible to say that if Christ was not raised from the dead with a body, Christians have been the victims of the greatest fraud in history and in all honesty should look for a more trustworthy religion.

So there is a crisis within Christianity as it faces Islam and it needs to be faced and resolved as quickly as possible. What is needed is a true 'fundamentalism'. Originally coined to denominate Christians who still believed in such 'fundamentals' as the virgin birth and the bodily resurrection of Christ, it has become a pejorative and contemptuous epithet for those who apply a 'literalistic' interpretation to everything in the Bible and apply it accordingly. I recall the comments of Richard Holloway, Bishop of Edinburgh and Primate of Scotland, in a review of one of my books. He said of my teaching: 'He is absolutely right. That's what the Bible says, along with a lot of other stuff we have long since discarded. Mr Pawson's difficulty is tragic. He is a good and kindly man and a fine Christian leader, but he is absolutely hung up on a fundamentalist method of scriptural interpretation. It makes him consistent, or as consistent as scripture, but he believes in doing what he thinks the Bible tells him to do . . .' I am saving these comments for the poor person who has the thankless task of writing my obituary! But they highlight the vulnerable weakness among us.

What is needed is a new fundamentalism, which takes the Bible in its entirety very seriously, searching for the meaning of every bit of it that was intended by the original writers and the Holy Spirit who inspired them, sticking strictly to what is already in scripture and can be brought *out* of it (exegesis) and avoiding reading *into* it what we think it says or would like it to say (eisegesis). In a word, it means accepting the Bible as presenting absolute truth, both in the events recorded and the ethics required (the latter in the New Testament for the Christian). Since all absolutes have opposites, the scriptures present clear alternatives: truth versus lies, light versus darkness, life versus death. It is all black and white, devoid of any shades of grey, and not open to negotiation. 'Let God be true, and every man a liar' is its stark demand.

Christians will need to be absolutely sure of such absolute truths as that the God of the Bible is the *only* one who really exists (Isaiah 45:5), that Jesus is the *only* way to the Father (John 14:6) and that salvation is found in no-one else (Acts 4:12). Only those who are so convinced that they are willing to suffer and even die rather than deny them and determined to propagate them by lip and life at every opportunity will be shown to be genuine Christians, likely to convert even their enemies.

To some this may come across as sheer arrogance and it has to be admitted that some Christians leave that impression. But it is not so much that 'we have the truth' as 'the truth has us'. We were proud rebels until we were confronted with the truth and had to give up our cherished notions in the face of it. We were persuaded to face the truth about ourselves in the light of the truth about God and it was a humbling experience that killed our pride but set us free to be real people with a real God.

I will finish by suggesting a novel but appropriate creed for Christians to recite, to themselves or with others. It summarises the most important articles of faith in the current situation and the most significant differences from Islam.

There is no god but Yahweh and Yeshua is his son.

* * *

If you prefer Anglicised versions of the Hebrew names, you can substitute 'Jehovah' and 'Jesus'. Either way, this expresses what Christians must be ready to live and, if it comes to that, die for, because it is the absolute truth and the ultimate reality.

9

Relationship

'Christianity is a relationship, not a religion.' This has been said so often that it has become a cliché. But it is nonetheless true, though it is not the whole truth.

Dictionaries define religion as 'belief in or worship of a supernatural power or powers considered to be divine or to have control of human destiny and any formal expression of such belief'. By that yardstick, Christianity is certainly a religion and it shares with other religions features such as worship, prayer, fasting, giving and moral standards for life.

Perhaps it is more accurate to say that Christianity is a religion based on a relationship. The Bible offers human beings 'abundant' life here and 'everlasting' life hereafter, but defines its essence as 'knowing' the only true God and knowing Jesus his Son (John 17:3). The biblical use of the word 'know' is far more than being informed about someone. It means to be intimate with someone (Adam 'knew' Eve and she conceived and gave birth to Cain).

Without such a relationship, Christianity loses its heart and soul. Alas, it can still be outwardly practised in a formal way – worship attended, prayers said, creeds recited, money given, decency and respectability upheld, etc. But the whole point of it has been lost and such nominal adherence, which I prefer to call 'Churchianity', is not likely to survive for long in a secular society, especially if that also involves some suffering. Moreover, Christians under persecution, robbed of Christian fellowship and even their Bibles, have been sustained by the relationship when unable to fully practise their religion. One thinks of Richard Wurmbrand in his Romanian prison or Corrie ten Boom in her German concentration camp, and thousands of others.

How is such a relationship possible? The answer is complex, so we must tease out a number of strands.

A HUMAN GOD

The first thing is that he is the kind of God we can understand, not fully but sufficiently to feel we can get to know him. The God of the Bible is surprisingly 'human', not because he is like us, but because we are like him, made in his image. He has shared with us the thoughts of his mind, the feelings of his heart and the intentions of his will. Even though he is 'Spirit' and without a physical body, scripture does not hesitate to talk about his face, eyes, ears, mouth, nostrils, arm, hand, finger, feet and even sperm (1 John 3:9, in case you don't believe me). Even our physical organs correspond to his spiritual functions. Such analogies are described and often dismissed by sophisticated scholars, influenced by Greek philosophy, as 'naïve anthropomorphism' (thinking of God as a human being); but they usually end up with an impersonal God who is much less real.

Even more significant, the Bible presents this very 'human' God in dynamic interaction with human beings. They respond to him and he responds to them. The biblical picture of our

120

relationship as clay in the potter's hand has been widely misunderstood and misapplied, the clay having as much influence on its final shape as the potter (Jeremiah 18). When we repent of (rethink and renounce) our sin, he repents of his punishment. He will even change his mind in response to human pleas, as both Moses and Amos discovered, which gives prayer a very different significance. The Bible is full of two-way conversations, even arguments (though he always wins, as Habakkuk found out).

Supremely, in Jesus, God really did become one of us. This was God with a human face – and indeed a whole body. God was no longer beyond our imagination but well within our comprehension. Jesus could say: 'Anyone who has seen me has seen the Father' (John 14:9). 'The Word became flesh' (John 1:14), made in our image, in the 'likeness' of physical, sexual, Jewish, male and even sinful flesh (Romans 8:3). When the Son of God became the Son of man (his favourite title for himself), not only was divinity incorporated into humanity, but also humanity was incorporated into divinity. God could never be the same again. There was a before and after in his own divine being. Humanity had been outside his being: now it is right inside. So much for the changeless God outside time!

Even where God is most unlike us, his being three persons in one, this helps rather than hinders our relationship with him. At a profound level, our God *is* a relationship, always has been and always will be. Sharing far more than three human persons ever could, Father, Son and Spirit present us with a perfect relationship of mutual respect, harmony and consideration that is an ideal for us to admire and emulate, even down to willing submission (Spirit to Son and Son to Father) of wife to husband, child to parent, employee to employer and all Christians to one another (Ephesians 5:21–

6:4). God himself is proof that perfect relationships are possible in our world and furthermore, has done everything possible and necessary for us to have them too.

He actually wants to have a relationship with us. He wants us to know him as well as he now knows us (and he knows the number of hairs on our heads). He wants us to share the perfect relationship he has within himself with each other as well as with him. As we have already explained, he created us because he enjoyed the company of his only Son so much that he set his heart on a larger family.

AN IMMANENT GOD

The whole point of our existence is that we are here to 'seek, reach out and find him' (Acts 17:27). Nor is this a tedious or arduous quest. In Jesus he took the initiative, came looking for us and got as close as he could without forcing himself on us. As Paul puts it, we don't have to find our way into another world, either heaven above or hades below; that is, we don't have to wait until after we die to find him. He is so near to us in this life, as near as outward speech on our lips or inward impulses in our hearts, so near that a simple but sincere cry for his saving help puts us in touch immediately (read Romans 10:1–13). There is, however, a prior condition: that 'anyone who comes to him must believe that he exists and that he rewards those who earnestly seek him' (Hebrews 12:6).

In all this one cannot help making a comparison between this God and the Muslims' Allah, highlighting a sharp contrast between them. Once again, the real question is not whether a person believes in God (or not) but what kind of God they do (or do not) believe in. Looking out over a calm

122

sea and a clear starlit sky, an officer on the bridge of a ship said to his captain: 'It's easy to believe in God on a night like this,' only to get the riposte: 'Yes, a God who is as cold as that sea and as far away as those stars.'

Allah is an isolated god. Back in 'timeless' eternity, he existed all by himself, all alone. Even after creating us, he is still without a peer group he can both love and be loved by, hence love is neither his name nor his nature. Nor does he reveal any hint of loneliness or having a desire for loving relationships.

Allah is a remote god. He is up in heaven rather than down on earth, 'transcendent' rather than immanent ('Immanuel' meaning 'God-with-us' is not one of his ninety-nine names). To use philosophical terms, already explained, Islam is deistic rather than theistic, a god who made the world including everyone and everything in it, but who does not intervene in our everyday affairs. He doesn't need to because all events are already decreed by his predestinating sovereignty and all we can and ought to do is 'submit' (the meaning of 'Muslim') to what he has already ordained.

Allah is a silent god. He used to speak to human beings, a select few called 'prophets', and then often indirectly, through an angel sent from heaven to earth. But he is now mute, as far as we are concerned, not having spoken for the last fourteen centuries, since his final message through Muhammad. Prayers may be said to him but he is not expected to answer in the form of a verbal reply. It is a one-way conversation.

Allah is a divine god. And that is all that can be said, the beginning and end of it. He is therefore very different from us, difficult for us to imagine or clearly understand. We can only submit to his revealed will in the hope of avoiding hell and attaining 'Paradise', but even that will have other pleasures than the delight of his company. True love and friendship partly depend on how much is shared in common by the persons concerned.

Having made these points, which I stress are all speaking comparatively, many Muslims, particularly in the Sufi branch, believe that a more personal, even intimate communion with the divine must be possible. They long and search for such a relationship, mostly in the realm of mystical experiences. But their own religion cannot offer them this, for a very simple reason. It neither tackles nor even seems aware of the real problem blocking such a relationship and therefore offers no adequate solution to it.

Islam acknowledges *a* problem, but it is a simple one. Human beings are born in a state of innocence and submission to the divine will; and are therefore naturally 'Muslim'. But most turn to their own will for life's decisions, proudly asserting their independence (the popular song: 'I did it my way' springs to mind). The answer to all our problems is an effort on our part to know and to do the divine will, as it has been revealed through his messenger, Muhammad. That we are fully capable of and responsible for such obedience will be seen on judgement day, when our 'good' deeds will be weighed in the balance against the bad. Yet even if the wrong scale tips, we can still nurse the hope of leniency since he is compassionate and merciful, though we can't bank on it.

However, even when all has been conscientiously observed, it does not seem to lead to a relaxed, much less a rejoicing relationship. The tone is still serious, even sombre, due to the lack of assurance of divine benevolence. By contrast, music is an integral part of Christian worship, needed to express the sheer happiness of being in the company of God and his family; not only do worshippers sing for joy but so does the

One worshipped (Zephaniah 3:17) – and the angels join in. Such celebration is the result of the real problem being diagnosed and remedied.

So why is it such a difficult thing for people to be in such a good relationship with their Maker? Why does it not come naturally? Why does there seem to be such a gulf between him and us? Why is it so hard to cross, so hard to bridge? Why does he not feel real or relevant? Why does he feel so distant?

A GOOD GOD

The Christian answer is very different. While acknowledging 'metaphysical' difference – he is divine and we are human; he is heavenly and we are earthly; he is spirit and we are flesh; he is infinite and we are finite – the real barrier to relating lies elsewhere, in a difference of attitudes rather than attributes, character rather than constitution. Christians agree with Muslims that the difficulty lies in the moral rather than the metaphysical realm, but at a much more profound level, needing a far more radical remedy than a disciplined change of behaviour. Indeed, Christians simply don't believe the gulf can be bridged from our side, even by 'superhuman' effort.

In a word, the problem is incompatibility, with which many married partners are only too familiar. Few realise how acute this is when we try to relate to God. There is that in divine nature which is contrary to human nature and vice-versa. There are traits in each which cannot mix, as different as chalk and cheese.

Putting it at its simplest: God is good and we are bad. It is not easy for a good person to befriend a bad person and it gets harder the better one is and the worse the other. So how 'good' is God and how 'bad' are we? Is the difference of degree (better and worse) or of kind (best and worst)?

'Good', like 'love', is an over-used word in English, to the point of losing any accurate meaning: 'good dog', 'good meal', 'good weather' right through to 'good man, or woman' and 'Good God!' (though the latter expletive verges on blasphemy). In its absolute sense of being entirely good, free from anything bad, it can only be used of God. When someone used this adjective to address Jesus, he immediately responded: 'Why do you call me good? No-one is good – except God alone' (Mark 10:18). He was really asking: 'Do you think I'm really good and are you thinking I am really God?'

The God of the Bible is a person of absolute purity and integrity. He must be true to his nature and all his behaviour will be consistent with it. There are therefore many things he simply cannot do, like telling a lie, breaking a promise, 'losing' his temper (though his anger is more fearsome because it is so controlled and directed) and above all, he cannot overlook sin, vice and crime in others. It is impossible for a God of unalloyed goodness to remain indifferent to or do nothing about the badness in others.

A JUST AND MERCIFUL GOD

This faces him with a profound problem. How should he treat those who spurn his love, break his laws, arouse his wrath, pollute his world, destroy his children and deserve his punishment? To a much lesser degree, many parents face the same problem with rebellious, obstinate and wilful children, showing no gratitude for the parental care they have received; but the problem is most acute for God because he is both just and merciful.

For us justice and mercy are usually in conflict. To spank or not to spank; that is the question. To punish or to pardon wrongdoing is the dilemma. We cannot exercise justice without compromising mercy or vice-versa. But God must do both to be true to his just and merciful nature. He can't just 'forgive and forget', as many would like him to do. To overlook wrongdoing like this, without punishing, only encourages it to continue. Justice must be satisfied in a moral universe, but so must mercy in a loving one.

The Bible tells us how God solved the dilemma. Scripture is often treated as if it is a compendium of answers to *our* problems (you know the approach: if lonely, read Chapter X; if depressed, read Chapter Y; etc.). But it is really about God's answer to *his* problem and it is most ingenious, to say the least!

First, his justice decided that the appropriate punishment for those who took a destructive attitude to themselves and others, to his creatures and his creation, was to limit their time on earth so that they should not go on spoiling things and frustrating his purpose permanently. In simple terms, sinners do not deserve to live for ever. They deserve to die. So death is not 'natural' for human beings, which is why we hate it, putting it off for as long as we possibly can. It is a judicial sentence on the way we live.

How then can justice demand death, and mercy cancel it, for the same person? They can't. But God is willing to accept the death of an innocent life in place of the guilty as adequate compensation to 'atone' for the wrong and thus satisfy justice and allow the guilty to be set free. The innocent dies and the guilty lives. In other words, 'without the shedding of blood there is no forgiveness' (Hebrews 9:22).

This principle of sacrifice for sin runs right through the Bible but has a very different practice in the Old and New

Testaments. God taught it to the Jews in a simple way by teaching them to kill animals, carefully selected for a flawless body, to 'atone' for their sins. That God accepted these offerings and sacrifices was a concession since he knew an animal was not an adequate substitute for a human being, not least because it was not voluntary but more because it was not morally perfect, even if without physical blemish. What was needed was a sinless human being who would willingly submit to death on behalf of sinners. But where was such a person to be found?

The human race could never have produced such a one. Far from being born in a state of innocence, we seem to have been born with a propensity towards the bad and a prejudice against the good. Even actors prefer bad parts, finding it much harder to play a convincing good role. We seem to be gripped by a law of moral gravity. However hard we try to escape its pull, none of us has yet succeeded. We are all fundamentally flawed and therefore unqualified to atone for each other. We may save others from death, for a time, by making the 'supreme sacrifice' out of devotion to them, but all we have achieved is a postponement of their sentence.

Only God could provide such a person and he did, by sending his only Son into our world. He came voluntarily, choosing for our sake to become a human being just like us, to be born in humble circumstances, to accept a low social status and simple lifestyle. But his primary purpose was neither to teach a nobler way of life nor set an example of it, though he did both. It was certainly not to start a new religion, though that has been one result. It was to restore a relationship between God and the human race by offering himself as a sacrifice in their place and on their behalf to 'atone' for all their sins.

He came to die and did so at an early age, at less than half normal life-expectancy. He arranged the time, place and cause of his own death by challenging the bad people so disturbed by his goodness. It was a public, painful and humiliating execution, the worst punishment for the worst criminal, and even his executioners acknowledged a gross miscarriage of justice. And God did nothing to stop it! In fact, God had planned it as the only answer to his own problem. On the basis of justice having been satisfied, God could now acquit the guilty, he could 'justify' himself as well as them, he could forgive them and restore the broken relationship, accepting them as if they had never been estranged from him.

His conditions for forgiveness had thus been fulfilled but there were some on our side of the transaction to be met. Though Christ's atoning death was sufficient for the whole human race, it would not become efficient for any member of it without their response and co-operation. The two basic requirements on our part are repentance and faith. Repentance involves thought (examining ourselves in the light of God's standards and realising how wrong we've been), word (naming our sins to him) and deed (cutting out what has been wrong and putting right what can be put right). Faith involves trust (being convinced that Jesus has taken our sins on himself) and obedience (doing whatever he tells us, the very first of which is to be baptised).

Yet all this only solves half of God's problem. A relationship has been restored. A person has been forgiven for the past, justified in God's sight, adopted into his family and able to call him 'Father'. But God still hates sin, while loving sinners. The things that offended, angered and even disgusted him before 'conversion' will still do so afterwards and be equally effective in spoiling the new relationship.

But how can we prevent this happening? The answer is: *we* can't! Past habits can undermine resolve. We know our own weaknesses. We can so easily drift back into our old lifestyle, as 'a dog returns to its vomit' and 'a sow that is washed goes back to her wallowing in the mud' (2 Peter 2:22; the previous verse states categorically that 'it would have been better for them [backsliding believers] not to have known the way of righteousness, than to have known it and then to turn their backs . . .').

However, God has solved this part of his problem as well, knowing we needed to be saved from the future power of sin as well as its past guilt, needing a Lord who would live for us as well as a Saviour who would die for us. So after allowing him to make the supreme sacrifice to purchase forgiveness for us, he raised him from the dead almost immediately afterwards, incidentally reversing the human verdict at his trial ('too bad to live') and giving his own divine verdict ('too good to let his body rot in the grave'). Evangelicals particularly need to be constantly reminded that his crucifixion without his resurrection cannot 'save' us from our sins (1 Corinthians 15:17).

> For if, when we were God's enemies we were reconciled to him through the death of his Son, how much more, having been reconciled, shall we be saved through his life!
> (Romans 5:10)

When Jesus was here on earth, the effect of his sinless presence was extraordinary. People found it impossible even to contemplate sin while he was with them. The better they knew him the more they longed to be like him. Temptation shrivelled in his company. Prostitutes and racketeers gave up their wrong ways after encountering him. Let readers ask themselves how they would behave if they could see that Jesus was in the same room while they even thought of doing something they knew he disapproved of. One glance of his eyes would kill the fantasy.

But this is assuming a visible, even physical presence, which is simply impracticable for our needs. Even after his resurrection, Jesus was still an embodied person and could be in only one place at once (Emmaus or Jerusalem or Galilee, but never all three). Had he remained on earth, his life could have saved only a very small number of people able to stay close to him. It was necessary for him to leave and be replaced by someone not so limited in space, who could be with his followers wherever they went.

Enter the Holy Spirit, the third person of the Trinity, the 'other comforter' (much more accurately translated as 'stand-by', the Greek word literally means 'beside-called'), whom Jesus promised to send as his replacement. But he would be much more than 'alongside'. As spirit, he would come inside, not only to make the life of Jesus vividly real but actually reproduce that life in the character of the believer. After all, he had been the power behind Jesus' messages and miracles, having joined him after his baptism at the age of thirty. The human Jesus needed this supernatural ability but not the purity, which he already had. But we need both, which is what the New Testament is referring to when it speaks of the availability of the 'gifts' and the 'fruit' of the Spirit. The God who commanded us: 'Be holy, because I, Yahweh your God, am holy' (Leviticus 19:2; 1 Peter 1:16), has given us all the help we need to obey him, by offering to fill us with his *holy* Spirit. The penitent believer, to be free from sin, needs two baptisms: to be drenched in water and in Spirit, to be born again *out of* water and Spirit (John 3:5 and Titus 3:5; again, see my book: *The Normal Christian Birth*).

THE GOSPEL OF GOD

All this is a summary in broad outline of the Christian 'gospel', the 'good news' that we can be free from both the past guilt and future power of our sins, free to enjoy an unhindered and unreserved relationship with God, no longer wondering whether he will be just or merciful towards us, knowing he has been both, true to his unique nature. And we have been saved from our sins by all three persons in God, working together in perfect harmony but with different contributions and all for our sake. The God above us, the God beside us and the God within us has achieved what we could never ever have accomplished for ourselves. The bond between divine being and human being, both being corporate as well as individual, is complete. Earth and heaven have met in Christ and are now joined in love.

Quite simply, the Trinity lies at the heart of the gospel. Without this reality, the relationship disintegrates. Without this good news, religion becomes bad news, an extra burden to be borne, extra duties to perform, something we have to carry rather than something that carries us, emphasising what we need to do for God rather than what God can do for us.

There is no trace of all this 'good news' in Islam. Both justice and mercy are attributed to Allah, but he is left to choose between them. The tension between them is not resolved. He cannot be both at the same time, much less towards the same person. And no individual can be sure in this life which place Allah will choose for him to go to in the next (with the exception of those who die for the cause of Allah, by their own hand or others').

Forgiveness is thought of in terms of leniency rather than reconciliation, being let off charges by a judge rather than the eager embrace of a father's prodigal love for a long-lost son. Nor does Islam see the need for a sacrificial death to atone for a sinful life. Forgiveness of sins is believed to be possible without shedding of blood.

The Quran's treatment of Jesus is consistent with this. Acknowledging his sinless life, a favourable contrast to Muhammad who admitted his sins and asked for forgiveness like everybody else, there is no link between his moral quality and his qualification to be a sacrificial offering, hence no emphasis on his death. Indeed the Quran even implies that his crucifixion never took place and someone who looked like him was taken by mistake (one suggestion is Judas Iscariot). The resurrection is also omitted, though his ascension is not.

As for the Holy Spirit, 'it', not he, seems less real to Muslims than Satan and the evil spirits, an ever-present cause of trouble.

So what have Christians to offer Muslims that they cannot find in their own faith? In a word, the gospel! But whether they become interested in it and attracted to it will largely depend on a noticeable quality of relationship between Christians and their God. Islam challenges Christians to display this, but it must be a special kind of relationship.

It must be *personal*, which 'I' and not just 'we' have. A friend of mine was asked why he was so sure that Jesus had risen from the dead and immediately replied, quite spontaneously: 'Well, I was talking with him only this morning.' Such genuine testimony can play a major role in drawing attention to the gospel. What he has said to *me* and done for *me* can be impressive, if it is communicated in an artless and sincere way.

It must be *present*, not something that was real many years ago but has now faded. All relationships need constant cultivation, spending quality time in mutual communication.

Having been baptised in the Spirit is of little value if one is not being led, guided and empowered by him today. Too many testimonies focus on the distant past.

It must be a *priority*, coming before all other relationships, even nearest and dearest, the first call on time, money, energy and all our resources. Such loyalty is clearly seen only when choices have to be made between conflicting demands or when social pressures have to be resisted.

While at least an individual relationship, it will also be *corporate*, shared by other Christians both with God and each other. Harmony within the Trinity is to be made visible to the world through the Church. Our love for one another is a vital ingredient in commending our faith to the world (John 13:35), it is the visible proof that we are in a loving relationship with God (1 John 4:20). Centuries ago, early Christians amazed observers, who exclaimed: 'See how these Christians love each other!' The challenge to Christians today is to attract the same comment.

Enough said? Not quite. There are some aspects of a loving relationship, as in a marriage for example, that should not be exposed to public gaze but kept secret, not least to avoid mixed motives creeping in. Jesus warned against parading the 'devotional' side of Christian living, including the exercises of giving, fasting and praying (his mention of 'praying at street corners' came alive for me when I lived in Arabia). Such things should be done for the sake of the loved One alone.

We can go further and say that the impact of the public side of our relationship will largely depend on the quality of the private side. People quickly sense if a public show of unity between husband and wife is not matched and undergirded with a harmony between them when they are alone together.

If Christianity is a religion based on a relationship, its founder wanted the relational rather than the 'religious' aspect to be the visible part. But there was another vital element to this demonstration of the gospel – righteousness.

10

Righteousness

Judaism, Christianity and Islam are agreed on at least three things pertaining to righteousness. First, that God is righteous in himself. In a word, God is good. His character is one of moral integrity. His will is the primary source of all moral standards, what is absolutely right and what is absolutely wrong. He can think, feel, say and do no wrong. He can be relied on to do only what is right. There is nothing arbitrary or unjust in his judgements. As Abraham, to whom all three faiths look, said to God when pleading for the righteous minority in Sodom before its destruction: 'Will not the Judge of all the earth do right?' (Genesis 18:25). A God who did not always do right would forfeit his right and authority to judge those who do wrong.

Second, God requires us to be righteous. He has made every human being aware of the difference between right and wrong and the need to embrace the right and eschew the wrong. He has done this by giving each a conscience, which particularly acts in retrospect, producing a sense of guilt and shame when violated. This is his 'natural' law, internal to man. Like the magnetic north pole to a compass, its message can vary, according to social influence, but it is still generally reliable enough to point in the right direction. For example, almost all societies in history have condemned incest. To some, however, God has given further external guidance, as in the Ten Commandments, which adds greater responsibility as well as privilege to those receiving the revelation. His moral demands are supremely shown through the lips and life of Jesus, his Son and our Lord.

Third, God will punish the unrighteous. His judgement will be absolutely fair, according to the light that has been received, whether through conscience, commandments or Christ. This is the complete answer to those who imply injustice in God by asking: 'What about those who've never heard?' (see Romans 2:12–16). All have heard their own conscience, though who can claim to have always obeyed it? And most are more ready to apply it to others than to themselves, only too eager to condemn in them what they condone in themselves. There is coming a day of judgement in which all will be revealed. Because God is a righteous God, this is a moral universe. Sooner or later, sin, vice and crime must be paid for. No-one gets away with anything.

The fact that God is so patient, so slow to anger, not punishing wrongdoing immediately or even in this life, has lulled many into complacency, a false sense of security, a delay of which they take full advantage. They have completely missed the reason for his reluctance: to give them the chance to amend their ways. As far as Judaism is concerned, the punishment would come before death, in terms of temporal suffering. Islam and Christianity agree that while some consequences may occur in this life, the main penalty will be faced after death, in terms of everlasting torment in the fire of hell (though, as we have noted, many Christians are ignoring or even denying *Jesus' teaching* on this; Matthew

5:22, 29–30; 13:42; Revelation 14:11; 20:10; the latter are also 'the revelation of Jesus Christ', Revelation 1:1).

On these three points all these religions agree, but there the agreement ends and huge differences begin. There are two in particular, one a difference in degree, namely, the *standard* of righteousness; and the other, a difference in kind, namely, the *source* of righteousness.

STANDARD OF RIGHTEOUSNESS

The question is simple: How good do we have to be in order to 'pass', on that day when each of us renders our account on how we have lived? How stringent is the standard by which our lives will be measured? It is the key question in all religions.

Islam, by comparison, is the easier. For one thing, its moral requirements are comparatively few and are readily communicated and understood. They reflect the simple life of the desert environment from which they sprang fourteen centuries ago. They represent basic rules governing individual and communal life.

For another, they are well capable of achievement by ordinary people, given a degree of determination and discipline. Expectations are reasonable and attainable. Part of the appeal of Islam is that its demands are within the reach of average men and women, even if in practice they can be inconvenient, irritating and even irksome.

Above all, the standard used on the day of judgement will be relative, not absolute. The decision will be based on balance. 'Good' deeds will be put on one side of the scales of justice and 'bad' on the other. Whichever outweighs the other will decide the issue, though there is always the hope that a 'compassionate, merciful' God will give a little leeway if the bad side is not over-weighted. But the main thing is that the 'pass' mark is well below perfection. Fifty-one per cent is certainly acceptable and 49 per cent might be. Putting it simply, if we want to be sure of 'Paradise', we need to be more good than bad.

Judaism is considerably harder. Again, the laws given through Moses govern individual and communal behaviour. But there are so many of them, ten major ones, which 603 others expand and apply. Rabbinic exposition elaborates these in ever-increasing detail. The 'sabbath' law is a case in point. Even in Jesus' day they had reached ludicrous proportions, which he rejected as traditions of men rather than the word of God. Today there are bizarre distinctions between pressing an elevator button (which would come under the definition of forbidden 'labour') and climbing many flights of stairs (which would not)! Even ignoring such petty restrictions, the original, divinely inspired legislation is too complex for all but the totally dedicated. A 'sinner' is not necessarily a bad person, but simply someone who has given up trying to keep them all.

And keeping them all, all the time and in all places, is what the Mosaic law required and what the people of Israel agreed to as their part in the covenant made at Sinai (Exodus 19:5; 24:3), knowing that God would curse them if they didn't (Deuteronomy 27:26). There was provision for unintentional transgression (the 'atoning' sacrifices in Leviticus 4–5), but not for wilful and deliberate disobedience. Severe sanctions included execution for at least fifteen offences of individuals and the loss of land and protection for the whole people.

Contemporary Judaism faces the problem of having lost the temple, priesthood and sacrificial system. Even unintentional sin has lost its remedy. Its theology has been adapted to deal with this and is actually now nearer to Islam than Christianity. God can forgive sin without the need for atoning sacrifices. It is a bloodless act, requiring only repentance on our part. The annual 'Day of Atonement' (with its 'scapegoat' and blood of bulls and goats in Leviticus 16) has become a day of repentance. In Israel the chief rabbi lists the sins of the previous twelve months, which always includes the reckless road behaviour of a nation that learned to drive on tanks!

For all practical purposes, it has become a case of doing one's best and hoping that God's mercy can cope with the rest, not unlike the 'good outweighing the bad' approach. Some, of course, try much harder than others, but most Jewish people settle for a compromise that keeps conscience at bay. For many the Torah has become more cultural (circumcision, sabbath, kosher diet, etc.), aiming to preserve 'identity', rather than moral (to please God). But the covenant with God remains, as does the sheer impossibility of even the most devout to do all he commanded through Moses, a dilemma that lies at the heart of their religion.

Christianity is the hardest of all. Jesus is widely acknowledged as a great, even the greatest, moral teacher and it is widely admitted that if the world lived by his precepts it would soon be a much better and safer place in which to live. His 'Sermon on the Mount' (Matthew 5–7) is recognised as a supreme ethical blueprint for society, even by non-Christians such as the Indian Gandhi, and the Russian Dostoevsky.

However, at the same time Jesus' teaching has been dismissed as impracticable in anything but an ideal world, which this one is certainly not. It is said to be quite contrary to 'natural instincts', such as self-preservation, having little fruit except the burden of a deepening guilt complex in any who even attempt to meet his demands.

Take sex, for example, a major part of our make-up and an increasing feature of our public life, easily becoming an obsession in both spheres. Yet Jesus taught absolute chastity (no sex before marriage) and absolute fidelity (no sex outside a marriage). Criticising the Mosaic law for its concessions to human nature and its compromise of God's intention, he insisted on monogamy (one marriage to one person for life, until the death of one dissolved the union), thus condemning all polygamy, consecutive as well as simultaneous, and making all remarriage after divorce an adulterous affair (Luke 16:18).

Above all, he extended the scope of morality to include inward attitude as well as outward action. The sin of adultery includes glances of the eyes, even fantasies of imagination, which spring from lustful desires. The sin of murder includes words of contempt and thoughts of hatred. Clearly he was basing all this on the principle that what God sees he must judge. We may hide our innermost thoughts and feelings from others, but not from him to whom doing something inside in our imagination is the same as doing it outside in reality, the 'mental and emotional' being as real as the physical.

But there is a more profound principle behind even this. The morality expected of his creatures is that of the Creator. We are created in his image to live up to that image. Measuring our moral quality, by other people, especially those we consider 'worse' than ourselves ('I thank you that I am not like other men – robbers . . . adulterers', Luke 18:11), is dangerous because it is deceptive. Only by comparing ourselves with God can we assess ourselves accurately ('Go away from me, Lord; I am a sinful man!', Luke 5:8).

Jesus commanded his followers to 'Be perfect, therefore, as your heavenly Father is perfect' (Matthew 5:48), but he was only demanding what God had said before through his prophet Moses and would say after through his apostle Peter (Leviticus 19:2; 1 Peter 1:16). In other words, God is not only perfect, he is also a perfectionist and requires perfection in his creation and his creatures, though in their present state neither does or even can provide this for him. As with all perfectionists, imperfection is profoundly offensive, especially if others are responsible for it, ruining what left his hands in perfect condition.

We can hardly imagine what anger sin arouses in God, but the Bible does not hesitate to describe his reaction to the moral and physical pollution of our planet in terms of his wrath.

So what is he going to do about it? The answer is breathtaking! He's going to start all over again, dissolving this entire universe into the energy from which it was created (in 'fire'; 2 Peter 3:10) and creating a brand new outer space and planet earth (the meaning of 'a new heaven and a new earth' in Revelation 21:1, in contrast to 'the first' of Genesis 1:1). And it will be 'the home of righteousness' (2 Peter 3:13), from which pollution of all kinds will be excluded for ever. Nothing and no-one impure will ever even enter it (Revelation 21:27).

So what hope is there for us? Even if we went in as forgiven sinners, we'd soon spoil it for ourselves, for others and, above all, for God. If the prime purpose of the final day of judgement is to select a population fit to inhabit such a perfect place and the qualification is total righteousness (the pass mark no less than 100 per cent), then no Jew, Moslem or Christian, nor anyone else, can face that day with confidence or even faint hope. What point is there in trying to be good? Actually, none at all, if that's why we are making the effort!

Only those who have reached such a point of moral despair for themselves can really appreciate the difference in kind, as well as degree, between Christianity on the one hand and Judaism, Islam and indeed all world religions on the other. Not only its standard but also its source of righteousness is radically different.

SOURCE OF RIGHTEOUSNESS

Every religion, whatever its basis or objective, has a section of its teaching entitled: 'What you must *do*', leading on to: 'What you must *be*'. There is a basic appeal to self-effort, to self-discipline, and an assumption that human nature is capable of climbing to the heights of spirituality in the presented goal and is therefore responsible for success or failure. This may be qualified with an offer of some divine or supernatural aid but such help or assistance is supplementary to one's own energy and determination.

All this is 'do-it-yourself' (DIY) religion, self-help spirituality, in theological language, salvation by works. Even the Mosaic covenant in the Old Testament can be thought of in this way if its 'Do this and live' is separated from the redemptive liberation from slavery in Egypt. Islam falls firmly into this category: Righteousness is an attainable achievement. Holiness is human.

But there are two fatal flaws in this approach. The first is that self-help leads to self-righteousness. The more that is achieved, the worse it gets! It invariably encourages two offensive attitudes: *hypocrisy*, because the emphasis falls on the outward observance of the 'letter' of religious rules, while allowing the inward disobedience to their 'spirit'; *arrogance*, because the more we achieve, the prouder we are of ourselves and the greater contempt we have for others of lesser achievement and especially those who don't even try. Jesus encountered both hypocrisy and arrogance in the Pharisees, supreme examples of self-righteousness in his day. Hence his extraordinary demands of his own followers that their righteousness must *exceed* this sort (Matthew 5:20). Paul, who had been a righteous Pharisee, observing all the religious rules of Moses, looked back on this with utter disgust.

Self-righteousness is instinctively disliked by people, but it is an affront to God, who is the sort of person who humbles himself, even allowing himself to be publicly humiliated – supremely seen in his Son's incarnation and crucifixion, an attitude he expects in all of us (Philippians 2:5–11). This kind of God brings down the proud and exalts the humble. He will ensure that the 'poor in spirit' will have the kingdom of heaven and the meek will inherit the earth, the most radical revolution history will ever have seen.

It is no exaggeration to say that self-righteousness, especially when in religious dress, is more offensive to the God of the Bible than blatant sin, partly because it leads to self-congratulation, self-adulation and even self-worship, but also because it is so much harder for him to remedy. People who know they are bad are far more likely to welcome help than those who think they are good, which is why prostitutes seized Jesus' offer of the kingdom while Pharisees held aloof, eliciting his ironic comment: 'It is not the healthy who need a doctor, but the sick . . . For I have not come to call the righteous, but sinners' (Matthew 9:12–13; taking the Pharisees at their own estimation of themselves, though he saw them as 'whitewashed tombs', a spotless outside covering up a rotten inside).

The other even more fundamental flaw in the quest for a 'righteousness of their own' (as Paul calls it in Romans 10:3, applying this to Jewish religion) is that it can never achieve its objective. That is, *if* the only true God is the God of the

Bible and expects us to be as good as himself. The more one achieves the harder it gets and the further off the target seems to be. Only those who have really tried their very hardest, like the apostle Paul and the monk Luther, are overwhelmed with the hopelessness of their pursuit. Sooner or later, the donkey that cannot reach the carrot gives up in despair!

The Bible does not define wickedness as exclusively applicable to perverts, criminals and tyrants, as we tend to do. To be wicked is to be ungodly and unrighteous, described in terms of 'falling short of the glory of God' (Romans 3:23), that is, failing to reflect the full righteousness of God in whose image we were made. It makes 'no difference' (Romans 3:23 again) whether we 'fall short' by a few yards or many miles, any more than to a man on a rock cut off by the incoming tide attempting to jump to the safe shore. We are still unrighteous by God's standards, unfit for his planned new universe.

One thing is clear. The source of the righteousness he requires cannot be found within human nature. It is universally acknowledged that 'No-one's perfect' or ever can be. This observation may calm our consciences but cannot satisfy God's. The situation is hopeless, unless . . . we could find another and adequate source outside ourselves.

The Christian 'gospel' or 'good news' meets this very need. At its heart is the discovery that there is such a source available, not within human nature but within divine nature. Incredible though it sounds, we can actually tap into *his* righteousness! That is why Paul is not ashamed of the gospel; confident that it can save us from all our own unrighteousness precisely because in it 'the righteousness of God is revealed' (Romans 1:16–17). Note that he does not begin with the love of God, which always comes later.

In expanding on this, Paul, surprisingly and even paradoxically, goes straight on to his implacable hatred of unrighteousness and his holy anger (wrath) against it. But, as the missionary statesman Bishop Stephen Neill, rightly pointed out: 'The gospel has to be bad news before it can be good news.' Like jewellery best displayed against a black cloth, God's anger against all that is bad in us is the obverse side of his goodness, proof that he is righteous.

His anger is visible to us ('revealed from heaven') in two phases. Like a pan of milk on a hot plate, there is a simmering as it warms up, with small bubbles coming to the surface, unnoticed unless carefully watched, followed by a sudden and often unexpected boiling over, with devastating effect. At present we can see his anger simmering in such things as increased homosexual activity and many other examples of antisocial behaviour, especially those that undermine marriage and family life (for a full list, read Romans 1:18–32 alongside a Sunday tabloid newspaper). One day his anger will boil over; it is called 'the day of his wrath' in the New Testament. All unrighteousness will be drastically dealt with, but since there is no such 'thing', only unrighteous people, that will be a terrible and terrifying day for many.

This was as far as Martin Luther could get in his desperate attempt to become righteous before God as an ascetic monk, praying, fasting, even scourging himself. Thoughts of God's righteous anger filled him with dread. Then, as he both studied and lectured on Paul's letter to the Romans, the truth burst on him that God was revealing his righteousness to us in an altogether different way, a welcome and wonderful manner that fills us with joy and gratitude.

In short, God is not demanding *our* righteousness *from* us, but offering *his* righteousness *to* us. Knowing perfectly well our complete inability to meet his requirements, he wants to meet them himself, both for us and in us, not by lowering his standards to us but by lifting us to them, not by becoming less than good himself but by making us as good as he is. The gospel is not so much 'You *must* be holy' as 'You *can* be holy'. This is great news, not just good news. Most people, in their heart of hearts, long to be better persons than they have become and they can now be told that it is well within their reach, not by trying but by trusting. I have seen the transforming power of this gospel from top-security prisons to gypsy encampments. That God wants to share his righteousness with us and set us free from the fruitless struggle to produce our own is the best news a human being could ever hear. His 'righteousness' is therefore bad news for those who want to be bad and good news for those who want to be good. And there will come a day when these two desires will be irrevocably fixed in two destinies (Revelation 22:11).

How does God share his righteousness with the unrighteous? How does he make bad people good? How does he turn sinners into saints? The answer is twofold and it is absolutely vital that both parts are held together and communicated together if the 'full gospel' is to have its intended effect.

God shares his righteousness with us by first imputing, then by imparting it to us, the one making the other possible. The technical terms for the two phases are 'justification' and 'sanctification'. In simple language, he first treats us as if we were good, then he makes us as good as he has treated us! Let me explain.

IMPUTED RIGHTEOUSNESS

We are caught in a vicious circle. God cannot share his righteousness with us if we are not in a right relationship with him, but he cannot be in a right relationship with unrighteous people. There can be no real relationship between perfectly righteous and patently unrighteous persons.

God has solved his own dilemma by initiating a relationship, by treating the unrighteous as righteous, declaring them to be 'in the right' (the meaning of the word 'justify', as when we defend an action such as spending money or coming home late). It was a legal term, originally used when a prisoner was declared innocent, could leave the court and return to his family in peace. Preachers have made some delightful attempts to explain 'justified'. One said it is God accepting me 'just-as-if-I'd' never sinned. I like the Pidgin English in New Guinea best: 'God, 'e say 'im all right.' This is, of course, forgiveness, always an essential element in restoring estranged relationships.

But isn't it all a legal fiction? A game of bluff? How can a God who knows perfectly well we are guilty pronounce us innocent? Isn't it immoral to treat wrongdoers like this? What would happen if parents and police followed this divine example? Who does he think he is kidding, us or himself? If God were simply 'letting us off', which is what many think forgiveness is, he would indeed be acting out of character, untrue to his own nature.

But it is none of this. He can only do so because the penalty has already been paid. Justice has already been satisfied. Atonement has already been made. An innocent life, freely given, has already been taken and accepted as a sufficient sacrifice for the sins of the whole world. A really good God simply could not accept the guilty as innocent until such an innocent had been accepted as guilty.

God has not compromised, much less contradicted, himself. Because of what his Son has done, the Father can welcome us back into his family. In choosing to become a man, to serve others at the point of their deepest need and to die young rather than live to be old, Jesus was fulfilling a condition that only a perfect human who was also divine could have met. Only because of his crucifixion is it possible for God to be both 'just and the one who justifies those who have faith in Jesus' (Romans 3:26); that is, whoever trusts him completely, to be who he said he is, to have done everything needed to free us from the past, to be doing everything needed in the present to maintain our standing before God and to do everything needed to secure our future.

There is still one other condition that can and must be met on our side before we can be forgiven, justified and 'reconciled to God'; namely repentance, which involves a right about-turn away from our sinful selves to a holy God, including a willingness to put whatever can be put right in his sight and under his direction.

Those who have done this are now 'in' Christ, as far as God is concerned. Our sinful past is unseen, 'covered' by his righteous life and death. 'Bold we approach the eternal throne . . . clothed in righteousness divine', as the hymn writer Charles Wesley put it. His righteousness has been 'imputed' to us because our unrighteousness has been imputed to him. The exchange may seem grossly unfair to us but to God it is completely just. We can only accept that in wonder and gratitude.

But the good news doesn't stop there. Alas, far too many Christians think it does. They are content with imputed righteousness, not realising that God is not. He needs to 'impart' his righteousness to us as well, if we are to be fit to live in that new universe he has planned. Holiness is as necessary as forgiveness (Hebrews 12:14). In theological terms, sanctification is as needed as justification for ultimate 'glorification' (sharing God's glory in a glorious future:

Hebrews 2:10). As the writer of the hymn 'There is a green hill far away' put it so simply:

> He died that we might be forgiven,
> He died to *make us good*. (My italics)

Why have so many Christians missed the point? It is partly due to misguided evangelists, whether speaking to crowds or individuals, who have virtually handed out tickets to heaven in response to a thirty-second repeated 'sinner's prayer'. By implication they have equated justification with salvation, though the former is a matter of moments and the latter takes a lifetime. The verb 'to save' is then used in the past tense ('I'm saved', 'I was saved ten years ago', 'We had three people saved last Sunday', etc.); though the New Testament uses it in three tenses: past ('We have been saved'), present ('We are being saved') and future ('We will be saved'), clearly indicating a process taking time rather than an instantaneous event.

Other symptoms of this misunderstanding are an excessive emphasis on Christ's past work (and more on his crucifixion than his resurrection), a misplaced location of his present work (in our hearts rather than in heaven, where he now is) and bringing forward his future work (going to heaven when we die rather than living in the new earth after we are judged). Above all, there can be a moral complacency that accepts continuous failure to overcome temptation, in spite of the Lord's promise to allow only those we are capable of resisting (1 Corinthians 10:13), an acceptance of a continuous cycle of sin, confession and forgiveness as the 'normal' Christian life, and thought of holiness as an optional extra, which could add a bonus of reward in heaven but is not necessary to secure our place there.

The situation has not been helped by the widespread cliché: 'Once saved, always saved'. By New Testament standards, even the first phrase is not yet fully true of Christians, much less the second. But it sums up a Protestant tradition of teaching going back through the Reformers to the Catholic Bishop Augustine, though it is usually labelled 'Calvinism' after its best-known exponent. Putting it crudely, salvation is seen as God's continuously moving assembly line. Once having got on it, it is impossible to get off until the product reaches completion. In theological language 'justification' inevitably must lead to sanctification and ultimately glorification, for nothing and no-one can resist God's absolute power (some even say he put you on the 'way of salvation' regardless of any choice or attitude on your part, his inscrutable 'election' appearing quite arbitrary to us). So, if you have been selected and justified, you are as good as 'saved' from all future as well as past sins. Hallelujah! Heaven, here I come. How come then, that so many start the Christian life but obviously don't continue, never mind finish? The Calvinist logic is simple: 'They were never truly saved', but were self-deluded. Is that really all that needs to be said?

Those taking a different view are generally labelled 'Arminians', after their best-known exponent, the Dutchman Jacobus Arminius, who studied under the Frenchman Jean Calvin in Geneva. Based on eighty passages in the New Testament warning about the danger of losing what we have found in Christ and even more exhorting believers to press on and 'make every effort . . . to be holy; without holiness no-one will see the Lord' (Hebrews 12:14), they do not believe that sanctification inevitably follows justification, or that forgiveness automatically leads to holiness. Both are choices dependent upon the human will, or rather, willingness.

Calvinists are prone to accuse Arminians of teaching justification by faith and sanctification by works, but this is a misleading caricature. Both justification and sanctification are 'by faith', the former by instantaneous faith and the latter by continuous faith (most uses of the verb 'believe' in the New Testament are in the Greek 'present continuous' tense, which means to 'go on believing', even in John 3:16).

However, both parties are agreed that we need more than imputed righteousness to satisfy divine intention. We need more than being *treated* as holy; we need to '*be* holy, as he is holy'. And the good news is that we can be, in the here and now as well as in the hereafter and then.

IMPARTED RIGHTEOUSNESS

In sharing his righteousness with us, God wants both to cover us and fill us with it, to give us forgiveness and holiness, to justify and sanctify us. And he is as capable of one as the other, given our co-operation. The writer of the famous hymn 'Rock of ages' was not presenting a hopeless request when he sang: 'Be of sin the double cure, Cleanse me from its guilt and power.' But he was highlighting the full problem of sin.

Forgiveness – justification – deals only with the past. It doesn't clean up the future by preventing further sin. The bad habits, mental and physical of our former life (scripture calls this our 'old man') are still there in our former nature (scripture calls this the 'flesh'), ready to trip us up or provide ground for the devil (scripture calls him a 'prowling lion') to get hold of us again. But none of this need happen.

God planned a double substitution. 'God made him (Jesus Christ) who had no sin to be sin for us, so that in him we might become (not just be covered by) the righteousness of

God' (2 Corinthians 5:21). What an exchange! He takes our badness and gives us his goodness. Has there ever been such a bargain? How sad that many are glad to have their sins loaded on him but reluctant to have his righteousness in return. But how does he give it and how do we receive it?

Enter the Holy Spirit. All three persons in God are both needed and involved in our being saved from our sins, their power as well as their penalty. But their functions are different, though complementary. Sanctification is particularly the work of the third person of the Trinity. Holiness is the product of his department. Indeed, he is the only one of the three for whom 'holy' is a part of his name and not just one of his character attributes.

He has been described as the 'executive of the Godhead' because he makes happen on earth what the heavenly Father wishes. He has been doing this from the beginning in nature (Genesis 1:2) and throughout history, in Israel's heroes (prophets like Moses, champions like Samson, kings like David), supremely in Jesus Christ and now in Christians. The Father is God above us, the Son is God beside us, but the Spirit is God within us. So far as I know, Christianity is the only religion which believes that the God we worship outside ourselves actually takes up residence inside ourselves.

Christians who have received the Holy Spirit are now free to choose between walking by the flesh (their old nature) and walking in the Spirit. That is, each step they take in life can be in response to the 'lust of the flesh' or the leading of the Spirit. As they respond to the latter, a wonderful thing gradually happens. A fruit grows in them, a single fruit with nine flavours – love, joy and peace in God; patience, kindness and goodness to others; and faithfulness, meekness and self-control for themselves (Galatians 5:22–3). All nine have never been found together in any human being except Jesus. The same Spirit whose power and purity enabled him to exhibit them is able to reproduce them in us. Would you love to be like Jesus? You now can be! That's the good news. The gospel is neither 'You must be righteous', nor 'You needn't be righteous', but 'You can be righteous'.

But it must be his righteousness, not yours. With this we come to the hardest bit, involving a severe blow to our pride. We need to renounce our righteousness to make room for his. Repentance involves turning away from our good deeds as well as our bad. They may have been of value to others but they are of no value to ourselves when seeking to be right with God. In fact they become a major hindrance if we trust them to get us at least part of the way. 'Do your best and leave the rest to God' simply does not work with him, though that is probably the most common misunderstanding about Christianity and the reason why many consider they can be as good a Christian outside the church as any inside. Even our best efforts are so much below God's standards that they are offensive to him and to us, when we see them through his eyes. Biblical writers use the crudest language to describe this insight. To the prophet Isaiah: 'all our righteous acts are like filthy rags' (Isaiah 64:6, the literal Hebrew refers to a soiled menstrual cloth or 'tampon'). To the apostle Paul, all his successful endeavours to keep all God's commandments he came to regard as disposable 'rubbish' (Philippians 3:8, polite modern versions where older ones have 'dung', though the Greek word is a vulgar reference to human excreta rather than animal, the nearest English equivalent being the Anglo-Saxon 'shit'). To present our good deeds to God to get his approval is like a small boy holding up his potty and saying: 'Look what I've done'!

As well as renouncing our own righteousness, which is so much easier for the renegade than the respectable, we need also to 'receive' the Holy Spirit, to be 'anointed' by him as Jesus was, to be 'filled' with him, to be 'baptised' (plunged, drenched) in him. The New Testament uses many synonyms for the rich and conscious experience of our first encounter with him. He is not, as many seem to think, inherent in human nature, residing in all human beings. He comes in response to being invited. Christ asked his Father to send him to us (John 14:16) and we also need to ask (Luke 11:13), being eligible for this wonderful 'gift' after we have repented of our sins and been baptised in water so that they may be forgiven (Acts 2:38–9).

Believing in the second person of the Trinity must not be confused with receiving the third. Even in the New Testament there are cases of one coming before the other, either with a brief or much longer gap (in Acts 8 and 19). Confusion arises because contemporary evangelists persist in using unbiblical jargon when counselling enquirers, such as: 'Receive Jesus into your life', 'Invite Jesus into your heart', 'Give your life to Jesus', 'Receive him as your Saviour and Lord', 'Make a commitment'. None of these euphemisms can be found in scripture and all leave the Holy Spirit right out, even though the Holy Spirit is the only person of the Trinity who can be 'received' on earth until Jesus returns. The apostolic counsel needs to be restored: 'Repent towards God the Father, believe in his Son the Lord Jesus Christ and receive the Holy Spirit.' To tell people to live the Christian life without introducing them to the Holy Spirit is not only frustrating but tormenting (for a full discussion of this vital point, see my books: *Jesus Baptises in One Holy Spirit*, Hodder & Stoughton, and *The Normal Christian Birth*, from the same publisher).

When will our sanctification be complete? When will we be perfect as he is perfect, righteous as he is righteous? The answer is clear: When Jesus returns to earth and gives us our new bodies, like his glorious body (which is still in its prime at thirty-three; resurrection bodies do not grow old and weak).

It would obviously be foolish to put an imperfect spirit into a perfect body, but that will not happen because 'when we see him we shall be like him, for we shall see him as he is' (1 John 3:2). We shall reflect him when we have eyes only for him.

My wife has a strong faith but there is one thing I try to teach that she finds hard to believe, bringing her to the brink of doubt. It is when I tell her that one day her husband will be perfect! Her reaction is to say that if she based her faith on experience (as many do) she would find it impossible to believe, but she bases it on scripture and clings to the promises of the Lord. I respond that I have to believe that one day my wife will be perfect. However, I admit she may have a bigger problem than I have in believing this. And there may just be another factor in her struggle:

The very next verse (1 John 3:3) goes on to say: 'Everyone who has this hope purifies himself, just as he is pure.' If we are *really* convinced that one day we shall be entirely holy, righteous, clean, pure, this will be evidenced by an eagerness to be so as soon as possible. Given that the divine resources to be so are readily available, the possibility is now as well as then. The challenging fact is that every Christian is as holy as they really want to be! If we are not righteous yet, it must be because we still enjoy being unrighteous, or because we fear the consequences of being righteous in an unrighteous society (2 Timothy 3:12).

It's as if a multimillionaire told you that when he died, all his fortune would come to you, but that meanwhile he had arranged for you to have as much of it now as you wanted or needed. Friends would doubt you boasting such good fortune if you showed no inclination to tap what was already available. Or what young man would spend no time with his fiancée because he would have her all the time after they were married? If we really want someone or something, we'll want it as soon as possible. It's as simple as that. Most Christians would *say* they look forward to being righteous in the next life but the proof that they really do is their pursuit of it in this. God's will is that we should be holy here and happy hereafter. At least the prayer was honest that said: 'Lord, please make me holy, but not just yet', but that was its only virtue!

So there it is. God the Father is determined to have a larger family of righteous children and has made it possible. God the Son, through his incarnation, crucifixion, resurrection, ascension and intercession, has brought sinners back into a real relationship with his Father, now theirs as well as his. God the Spirit works within them to make them just like Father and Son, who are so like each other. Sinners can become saints in character as well as title. And when that is done, there will be a brand new universe in which the whole new family can live, for ever and ever.

What a hope! Unbelievers may say that in terms of mockery and cynicism, but for believers it is a celebration of certainty. And the proof of it, to others even more than themselves, is to exhibit even now a righteousness that clearly exceeds that which is achieved by human nature at its very best. The challenge to do so is the core of Jesus' Sermon on the Mount (Matthew 5:16, 20, 48; etc.) and is facing us today through the rise of Islam.

11

Reconciliation?

The human world is rapidly shrinking and is already a 'global village'. Increased mobility and information technology have made us far more aware of and informed about other cultures and religions than ever before. Big cities in every nation are cosmopolitan, not least in the variety of restaurants and their cuisines.

Many view the resulting mix as a potentially enriching opportunity and welcome the wider choice in taste and preference. At the same time, the bewildering variety on offer can make sampling a passing fad for novelty and reduce a commitment of a lasting kind to any.

And there is always the danger of tension between those that are mutually incompatible and therefore exclusive, demanding a choice between them, which the modern world is extremely reluctant to make for fear of 'missing out', a crisis that is most likely to arise in the realm of religion. Far from admiring convictions held passionately enough to be willing to die for, contemporary society regards such as dangerous bigotry. 'Fundamentalist' had an original meaning that was positive – someone loyal to the fundamental tenets of their faith – but is now an epithet of abuse, negative in tone: someone who is violently opposed to other faiths or even other versions of their own.

In a society where differing cultures and religions live 'cheek by jowl', it is hardly surprising that tact and tolerance have moved to the top of the list of cardinal virtues. They hold the key to unity and harmony in a multicultural community. Indeed, they are essential to its survival, keeping the lid on potential flash-points of conflict not far below the surface.

Enter political correctness, relativism applied to social behaviour, which replaces commonly held moral boundaries as the cement holding us together. Anything or anyone thought to be fostering disunity or division between the cultural elements in contemporary society is breaking the new code of conduct. Recent legislation criminalising stirring up religious hatred is a case in point. A lack of clear definition gives a wide spectrum of application, from downright verbal abuse to any attempt to proselytise.

Even to suggest that any culture or religion is superior, implying that others are inferior, is regarded as deeply offensive. Dialogue between any must be based on the premise that both are equally valid and valued, equally 'true' for the participants; and its objective must be mutual enlightenment and acceptance.

One of the worst 'sins' in such a milieu has earned the label 'demonising'. In its non-religious sense it means to identify those with whom one disagrees as the source of all evil and the cause of all problems. In its more common religious sense it means to identify one's opponents as direct agents of the supernatural forces of evil opposed to the good God. One example is when Muslims call Israel 'the little Satan' and America 'the great Satan'. I have been accused of the same, in what I have spoken and written about Islam, indirectly reflecting on Muslims. Demonising is regarded as a naive ploy to settle a dispute by slandering an adversary, fostering contempt and revulsion.

Christians will recall that Jesus himself was subjected to this insulting treatment, when his miracles were ascribed to the power of 'Beelzebub, the prince of demons' (Matthew 12:24–32). He seems to have regarded this slander as more serious than any other sin, regarding it as not directed against himself but against the person whose power enabled him to do all his miracles. 'Anyone who speaks a word against the Son of Man will be forgiven, but anyone who speaks against the Holy Spirit will not be forgiven' (Matthew 12:32), possibly because they have so damaged the sensitivity of their own conscience that they are no longer capable of discerning their guilt or repenting of it. It is the only 'unforgivable sin', though this applies to all sins until they are truly repented of. Even when Jesus told his followers to forgive their brother's sins against them at least 'seven times a day', he added the vital condition 'if he repents' (Luke 17:3–4). So Christians need to be especially aware of the danger of committing a sin that Jesus took so seriously.

If 'demonising' is one of the worst vices in a multicultural context, the task of 'reconciliation' has become one of the best vocations. Society applauds those who work to bring estranged parties or groups together again, usually involving prolonged negotiations.

Christians often regard such a 'ministry of reconciliation' as inherent to the Christian calling, a necessary 'outworking' of their salvation (Philippians 2:12–13). They recall the congratulatory benediction of Jesus in the renowned Sermon on the Mount: 'Blessed are the peacemakers, for they will be called sons of God' (Matthew 5:9). The 'ecumenical' movement sprang out of a guilt complex over the deep denominational divisions within the Christian Church itself (Orthodox, Catholic and Protestant, to say nothing of the myriad splintering groups inside and outside the primary groupings). Christians are embarrassed by their own failure to be the answer to Jesus' prayer for their unity, which he clearly saw as an essential and visible proof to the world that they had found and were following him (John 17:20–3). What right have Christians to attempt to reconcile others when they have so miserably failed to achieve this among themselves?

Nevertheless, Christians feel they cannot and must not wait until their efforts for unity succeed inside the Church before they make the same endeavour outside in the communities in which they live. Both quests can and should be pursued simultaneously.

So how is this 'ministry of reconciliation' to be applied in the wider sphere, particularly in the growing confrontation between Christianity and Islam? Christians are faced with three possible courses of action in seeking to reconcile current differences.

ISLAM AND CHRISTIANITY

The real meaning of the word 'ecumenical', like the word 'catholic', is 'universal; worldwide'. While originally it was only used in negotiations for unity within the Church, it is taking on a wider meaning with the increasing contact with other religions. The pressure is to unite the world religions for the benefit of the human race and its delicate environment. Religious harmony is seen as a major factor in attaining peace and avoiding pollution.

The pressure is on to forget our differences, to establish

mutual respect, trust and confidence and to work towards the syncretism of faiths into one world religion to unite the race – though the latter is so far down the line that it is not very high on the agenda yet.

The relativist thinking we noted in Chapter 2 reinforces this trend. No religion is considered to have a monopoly of truth, which is more likely to be found in an amalgam of different spiritual insights, an inclusive synthesis of many rather than an exclusive assertion by one.

The mass media already refers to 'the faith community', covering all religions. The BBC programme *Sunday* invariably majors on the two largest, Christianity and Islam. As mentioned before, Prince Charles' intention to be known as: 'Defender of faith', not '*the* faith', is another straw on the water, coupled with his visits to mosques and commendatory speeches about Islam.

There seem to be five phases in the coming together of the two religions:

1 Joint discussion. Frank and honest dialogue is an obvious starting point, not least to promote accurate information and representation and prevent caricature and misunderstanding.
2 Joint statements. Agreements reached in matters of doctrine or ethics can be issued together, especially if they have a bearing on social and political issues.
3 Joint action. Lobbying responsible authorities is just one example, where injustice or inhumanity is ignored in public policy. This is now called 'co-belligerence', that is, banding together to fight a common enemy. The only time I have heard Prince Philip, Duke of Edinburgh, preach a sermon in church (St George's, Windsor), it was a call for the

world religions to unite in order to save wildlife and its natural environs.

4 Joint intercession. This involves gathering together to pray for a shared objective, while praying to different deities. One of the most publicised was the Pope's gathering religious leaders to pray for peace in the town of Assisi, formerly the home of St Francis.

5 Joint worship. Such services will include praise and prayer to the 'God' of Jews, Christians and Muslims, readings from the Old and New Testaments plus the Quran and all led by a team of rabbis, pastors and mullahs, a united 'clergy' of the three monotheistic faiths, the underlying premise being that all three are worshipping the same God, however differently they think or speak of him.

One of the difficulties facing and dividing Christians is where to draw the line in this progressive sequence, which carries a momentum of its own and can take sincere believers from one stage to the next almost without realising it. Given the unpopularity associated with not being willing to go further with a process already begun and the stigma attached to withdrawal, it is not surprising that some Christians shrink from being involved at all, while others are sucked into collusion and compromise, even against their own conscience.

Church leaders are not agreed on where to draw the line, which further confuses the members. The former Archbishop of Canterbury, George Carey, set his seal on dialogue by inviting national Muslim leaders to Lambeth Palace for consultations, the last time just before he retired from office. The Director of the Evangelical Alliance is already advocating 'co-belligerence'.

Co-operation can seem to be rather one-sided. Memorial

services following the '9/11' tragedy invited mullahs to speak in churches and their disassociation from the terrorists was greeted with relieved applause. I have not yet heard of Christian leaders invited to preach in mosques. This reflects a wider imbalance. Muslims are welcome to take advantage of Western freedom to practise their religion, build their mosques and even preach inflammatory sermons but such privileges are not reciprocal in Islamic countries.

But the real issue to be faced is how far Christians are compromising their faith by engaging in wider ecumenical activity, not by denying its distinctive beliefs but by playing them down in order to present a united front. Scripture commands us: 'And whatever you do, whether in word or deed, do it all in the name of the Lord Jesus, giving thanks to God the Father through him' (Colossians 3:17), an injunction impossible to keep when co-operating with Muslims, to whom Jesus is not Lord and God is not Father. Quite simply, Christians are forbidden to engage in any shared activity that compromises their knowledge of the God they serve and the gospel they preach.

As far as God is concerned, it is hoped that by now the reader is as convinced as the writer that Muslims and Christians are not worshipping the same God. The two are radically different and only one can be the true – that is, the real – God (John 17:3; 1 Thessalonians 1:9; 1 John 5:20).

There is a huge contradistinction between a 'god' who is one person all on his own and a 'god' who is three persons in perfect unity and harmony with each other. The significance of the Trinity for the Christian understanding of God cannot be over-emphasised. As we have already explained, the concept of a Father who *is* love is directly dependent on the Trinity, but is absent from Islam and even regarded as blasphemous idolatry in the Quran. Muslims can sometimes see the difference between their 'god' and ours more clearly than Christians!

The difference is impossible to reconcile. The two concepts contradict one another at the deepest level. They are incompatible. Three into one won't go, either mathematically or theologically! Whatever the 'oneness' of God means to the Christian, it can never refer to his personhood. The Trinity is non-negotiable. And there is a very practical reason for taking this inflexible attitude.

As far as the Gospel is concerned, it also stands or falls with belief in the Trinity. Without the personal work of Father, Son and Holy Spirit, there can be no salvation from sin, either its guilt or power. Forgiveness would be a legal fiction, compromising divine justice. Human nature would remain unchanged, a recycled universe forever beyond reach. Without the Trinity, there would be no good news, only bad news.

The only really good news in Islam is that anyone dying for the cause of Allah is guaranteed access to a sensual paradise immediately after death. For everyone else, the future remains uncertain until judgement day.

The word 'gospel' is unique to Christianity, found in no other religion, including Judaism. It was the announcement of this news (the meaning of 'preach' in the New Testament) that established the new faith so widely and quickly in the Roman Empire and is doing the same today at the fastest-growing points around the world, particularly in the 'two-thirds' world. What Paul called: 'the glorious gospel of the blessed God, which he entrusted to me' (1 Timothy 1:11) has now been entrusted to us and we dare not betray that trust.

Islam and Christianity cannot be reconciled. We must not attempt such a futile task or even allow any impression that we consider it possible, much less desirable. But what about reconciling Muslims and Christians?

MUSLIMS AND CHRISTIANS

There were Jewish and Christian communities in the Arabian peninsula at the time of Muhammad, some known to him personally. The earlier part of the Quran reflects his respect for them, as 'People of the Book'; that is, people who based their belief and behaviour on the recorded revelations of God through his messengers. Muhammad saw himself as the latest and last of this line of 'prophets', over two dozen of them stretching from Adam, through Abraham, Moses and Jesus to himself. He hoped Jews would accept him as their 'prophet' and Christians as their 'apostle'. He may not have been fully aware that some of his 'revelations' were contradicting their scriptures, since neither Old nor New Testaments had been translated into Arabic and in any case he could not read.

However, when they did not recognise him as the messenger who was completing and finalising their own revelation, he became increasingly hostile towards them, even slaughtering them in some of his skirmishes. None can be found in Arabia today, though some still survive in other Muslim countries, such as the Coptic Church in Egypt. When the contradictions with the Bible came to light, it was said to have been deliberately corrupted to prevent it from being a true record of its 'muslim' prophets' messages. Later parts of the Quran regard Jews and Christians as 'infidels' (unbelievers), friendship with whom must be discouraged.

For centuries following, Muslim–Christian relations were characterised by military conflict, as the new religion expanded by force. Christians responded in kind when they could, the most notorious being the series of 'Crusades', beginning 400 years after Muhammad. This call of the Pope to liberate sites of pilgrimage in the 'Holy' land led to the wholesale slaughter of Jews, Muslims and even Eastern

Christians (the taking of Constantinople, then capital of the Byzantine 'Christian' empire was hailed as a victory), the killing reaching a climax in Jerusalem when it was reached. Memories of this appalling episode have been kept alive through generations of Jews and Muslims, who do not hesitate to remind Christians of the atrocities committed in the name of Christ, though they conveniently forget their own reverse ones.

Relations between Muslims and Christians have never been good. There is, of course, a clash of cultures, which are very different, but past history has added fear and suspicion to the mix and prejudice has played a part. Mutual trust is often conspicuous by its absence.

It is part of a Christian's calling to be a focus of peace and harmony. It is a logical outworking of having been reconciled to God. Jesus called peacemakers 'blessed' and Paul told his converts: 'If it is possible, as far as it depends on you, live at peace with everyone. Do not take revenge' (Romans 12:18–19). Turning the other cheek may not halt aggression but it is more likely to than hitting back. Jesus was himself a model of non-resistance, though they still killed him.

There is certainly room for improvement in relations between Muslims and Christians, if only on the basis of being fellow human beings. Christians need to recognise and respect the 'image of God' in which Muslims were created, just as much as themselves. They must be willing to take risks to demonstrate this. I think of two men, personally known to me, examples of reconciliation in quite different ways:

Lynn Green, prominent leader in Youth With A Mission, organised a march of Christians through Muslim lands to Jerusalem, following the approximate route of the Crusades. The aim was to express repentance and seek forgiveness for the atrocities committed back then and demonstrate that there are Christians who disassociate themselves from such thinking today, seeking to follow Christ's teaching that 'My kingdom is not of this world. If it were, my servants would fight' (John 18:36; hours earlier, he had rebuked Peter for using a sword on his behalf).

Andrew White, Canon of Coventry Cathedral, was called on by both sides during the recent siege of the Church of the Nativity in Bethlehem. Trusted by the Israeli and Palestinian governments, he risked his life from soldiers outside and terrorists inside to negotiate an agreement that would end the slaughter and starvation. He was motivated by the only mediator between himself and God, the man Jesus Christ (1 Timothy 2:5).

Both of these were seeking, in different ways, to improve relations between people and peoples or, at the very least, preventing them from getting worse. We Christians should be eager to do whatever we can to reduce alienation by attempting to remove ignorance, misunderstanding, prejudice, bitterness, hatred and all other such things which keep people apart.

Turning foes into friends is a worthy end in itself, but it is also an essential means to another end, that 'ministry of reconciliation' for which Jesus commissioned his disciples in his last words to them before leaving this world.

MUSLIMS AND GOD

The first calling of Christians is to foster vertical rather than horizontal reconciliation. Our Saviour and Lord

has committed to us the message of reconciliation. We are therefore Christ's ambassadors, as though God were making his appeal through us. We implore you on Christ's behalf: Be reconciled to God. (2 Corinthians 5:19–20)

This vital task must be our top priority.

Of course the horizontal may, and in many cases must precede the vertical. Establishing good relations with people earns the right to ask them about their relations with God. My father, who in his spare time led over 12,000 people to Christ, advised all who wanted to emulate him: 'Never try to board a human soul until you have pulled alongside first.' Which is exactly what Jesus did, known as 'a friend of sinners' before he became their Saviour.

But the vertical must always be the central objective. Christians can be tempted to let it slip into second place or lower, because it can be more offensive and resented than bringing estranged people together. But the main reason for such a lapse is letting the temporal and temporary needs in this life override the far more important eternal needs in the next. It is to forget that the real hell facing people is not here but hereafter, to overlook that sinners are 'lost' and need 'saving', not just lonely and needing befriending or unhappy and needing cheering up. If the Church is to be true to its calling, it must offer far more than a religious version of the social services.

There is no emphasis on reconciliation with God in Islam. It is a call to submission (a Muslim is a submitted one), not an offer of salvation (a Christian is a saved one). One reason is that the Quran does not accept that the whole human race is in a state of alienation from God, from the 'original' sin of Adam to the actual sins of all his descendants. We are '*by nature* objects of wrath' (Ephesians 2:3; italics mine), deserving God's anger. Whether we acknowledge it or not, our greatest need is to be reconciled to God.

And this includes all Muslims. Their own religion cannot give them this. At an interfaith conference in India, each representative was asked in turn what his religion had to offer, which no other religion could match. The Christian simply said one word: 'forgiveness' and no-one argued with him! Other religions present a demand; Christianity presents an offer, a unique offer.

Christians need to be absolutely sure that Muslims need to be saved and can be saved before tackling what can be a delicate and even dangerous mission and will only then do it because 'Christ's love compels' (2 Corinthians 5:14). There must be no thought of persuading Muslims to 'convert' from their religion to ours. Our objective is to see them saved from their sins, reconciled to the God who made and loves them and becoming members of his family rather than 'our church'. It is entirely for their sakes, not ours.

Formerly, taking the good news to Muslims involved separation from loved ones, travel to distant lands and life in an unfamiliar culture. Now, we don't need to go to them. They have come to us, in great numbers. They live in the same city, town, street, even next door. This new fact faces Christians with the acid test of how genuine was their missionary concern when they gave money to send others overseas to spread the gospel on their behalf. Now they can do it themselves, with no expense at all!

Many Muslims coming to Britain are more open to the gospel than if they had stayed at home. Some are actually escaping from countries controlled by Islam. Perhaps most have come for economic reasons but they have come into a place where freedom of speech is the rule, which means freedom to listen as well. But they need to see as well as hear the good news, in signs as well as deeds. A friend of mine has led many to Christ by going to Muslim homes when he hears of any sickness, asking if he may ask Jesus to heal them (he's never been refused yet). No preaching, no leaving tracts or Bibles, no invitations to meetings, just a little miraculous help that whets their appetite to find out more.

It is not my place to tell readers 'how to win Muslims for Christ'. Others with far more wisdom and experience than I have written books or booklets for our guidance, particularly how to avoid the pitfalls of rushing in with blunt, tactless and ignorant approaches that can do more harm than good. Ask your local Christian bookshop.

Why are Christians not seizing this fresh opportunity? I fear that one major answer lies in the alarming discovery that followers of other religions, including Islam, can be far more devoted to them and far more willing to acknowledge and apply their faith in public than many churchgoers, to say nothing of the English tradition of keeping religion out of polite conversation! Their dedication intimidates us.

Once again, it is 'the challenge of Islam to Christians'. Would that it were the other way round.

Author's footnote:
I had written an appendix to discuss the thorny question of whether Christians should use 'Allah' when referring to the God of the Bible, particularly in dialogue with or evangelism of Muslims. I have decided not to include it, lest this highly controversial issue, which divides even evangelical Christians, distracts attention from the central message, which is addressed to those on both sides of the debate. I do, however, intend to deal with the subject, about which I have already been asked, in greater depth and detail, in an audio tape which will be available from Anchor Recordings (tel and fax 01233 620 958), under the title 'There is no god but Abba'.

12

Retribution?

What is the future of Islam? It is already the second largest world religion, claiming one fifth of the present population, though Christianity is the largest, said to cover one third. And it is also the fastest growing, at over four times the rate of Christianity, and therefore likely to catch up and even overtake in the relatively near future, becoming the dominant religion on our planet, with the greatest influence on world events. What happens in Britain will reflect this larger picture.

How long is this scenario likely to last? For the next few decades? For the rest of the twenty-first century? To the end of history?

Will Christianity survive or be swamped? Will its present rate of growth speed up or slow down? Will any other religion have a similar resurgence to present-day Islam and contend for the lead role?

Has the Bible anything to say about all this? The answer is that our scriptures teach us to read the future backwards. Christian hope always starts with the ultimate situation promised by God and then views the immediate and intervening state of affairs in the light of that outcome. This approach is a wonderful cure for depression and despair.

There have been many attempts to discern a pattern or purpose in world events through the ages as twenty-one major civilisations have come and gone. Five such 'philosophies of history' have vied for attention:

1 The *cyclic*. Of Greek origin and sceptical character, this believes that history is going round in circles, endlessly repeating itself and getting nowhere.

2 The *epic*. History is definitely moving on, never exactly repeating itself but on a rollercoaster of ups and downs, peace and war, boom and bust. Whether it will climax with an up or a down is anyone's guess.

3 The *optimistic*. The world will get better and better. History is on a rising escalator. Progress is inevitable. The twentieth century began with this, but a series of disasters, from the sinking of the *Titanic* to two hot world wars and a cold one, have severely shaken this confidence.

4 The *pessimistic*. The world is getting worse and worse, with little or no hope of it getting any better. The twenty-first century is more concerned about survival than advancement and its first few years have witnessed major blows to peace and prosperity.

5 The *apocalyptic*. The world will gradually get worse and then suddenly better and stay there. This view is shared by Jews, Communists and Christians, who all got it from the same source, the Hebrew prophets. But they strongly differ in what will cause the sudden reversal in trend – Communists trusting in people, Jews in God and a man (the Messiah), Christians in a man who is God (Jesus).

When the Bible deals with the ultimate future, as in Daniel

and Revelation, it always adopts this 'apocalyptic' view (the Greek word means simply an unveiling of what has hitherto been hidden from view, but which has been unveiled; i.e. the fifth view listed above). Both Testaments teach us to look beyond an increasingly grim present to an impressively glorious future. With sovereign power God can use even evil forces to serve his good purposes, but they will also be judged with strict justice when their day is over and the 'day of the Lord' takes over. Judgement is an essential element in an apocalyptic future and will be completely impartial.

Take Habakkuk, for example. We have already looked at one side of his dialogue with God, his pessimism when God said he was bringing the Babylonian might to deal with the sorry state of his chosen people. The prophet was convinced this would mean the total extinction of Israel and tried to persuade God that such a drastic remedy would leave him with nothing, even suggesting that he was too good to let such bad people wipe out his own people (Habakkuk 1:13).

The prophet, however, was overlooking God's righteousness or, rather, thinking he understood it better than God himself did! So God reminded him that his righteousness would do two more things in the future. First, he would make sure that the righteous would survive by keeping faith. Second, he would deal with the unrighteousness of the Babylonians – in their case, idolatry, immorality and inhumanity – after he had used them. They were an instrument in his hands but he was under no illusions about them. It was these two reassuring reminders that enabled Habakkuk to sing and dance for joy, even before the disastrous invasion happened. The ultimate outcome outweighed the immediate prospect for him.

The ruins of Babylon, south of Baghdad in modern

Iraq, are mute testimony to God having kept his word. Rediscovered in the nineteenth century by archaeologists, mainly British, it was partly rebuilt by Saddam Hussein in the twentieth century, with his name and image deliberately alongside those of Nebuchadnezzar, comparing profiles. What was once the greatest city of humanity, from the Tower of Babel, along with one of the 'seven wonders of the world' – the 'Hanging Gardens' – Babylon is still uninhabited and one of the most desolate places on earth. Set alongside that the vibrant State of Israel, prospering in the land God promised to the Jews 4,000 years ago and from which most of them have been separated for 2,000 years. Habakkuk need not have worried. As the German poet put it:

> Though the mills of God grind slowly,
> Yet they grind exceeding small:
> Though with patience he stands waiting,
> With exactness grinds he all.
> (Translated into English by H. W. Longfellow)

Was it coincidence or providence, intuition or inspiration, that led me to repeated reference to Habakkuk as I meditated on the intrusion of Islam into the United Kingdom? Certainly I came to the conclusion that God would use it to refine his people in Britain, leaving those who are righteous by keeping faith. Was the analogy meant to include retribution as well as refinement, for his own people first, with whom his judgement always begins, for Christians as well as Jews (1 Peter 4:17), and then for others who he has used for that?

However, there is much more direct ground in the New Testament for thinking that Islam will not have the last word or the final pre-eminence in the annals of human history.

Analogies drawn from the history of Israel are not necessarily conclusive for the Church.

Of course, Islam is not mentioned by name in scripture. It arose centuries after the New Testament was written. But there are clear and numerous predictions about events at 'the end of the age', through which we can at least ask how Islam will fare. Surprisingly, the Quran also predicts them, while giving a very different meaning and purpose to both.

In a word, world history will climax with the successive rule of two autocrats, the first extremely malevolent but the second equally benevolent, the first very brief and the second quite prolonged, in a ratio of seven to a thousand. One will be inaugurated by the coming of the antichrist and the other by the second coming of the Christ.

THE ADVENT OF THE ANTICHRIST

Both Islam and Christianity anticipate a human puppet of the devil appearing on the earthly scene. Both Muslims and Christians are prone to identify his profile and ascribe his title to contemporary adversaries, usually to someone in the other religion but occasionally within their own (Luther and the Pope thus mutually identified each other in this way!). Certainly some autocratic figures have foreshadowed this character but as yet none has fulfilled or 'filled full' the predicted monster (or, in biblical terms: 'beast'). As the apostle John writes: 'you have heard that the anti-christ is coming, even now many antichrists have come' (1 John 2:18).

It is important to note that the prefix 'anti' means 'instead of' rather than 'against'. He will come in a Messianic role, with benign appearance. The first part of his strong rule will bring a real measure of peace and security to a world longing for it (dictatorship usually succeeds where democracy fails). However, the beneficial use of absolute power will quickly degenerate into totalitarian exploitation and repression. Hitler's rule in Germany's 'Third Reich' is just one example of these two phases; after dealing with inflation, unemployment and civil unrest, he turned to mass murder, both inside and outside his country.

The second half of his 'reign' is referred to as 'The Big Trouble', or 'The Great Tribulation'. As Jesus put it: 'Then there will be great distress, unequalled from the beginning of the world until now – and never to be equalled again' (Matthew 24:21), picking up Daniel's ghastly description of this offensive creature as 'the abomination of desolation' (Matthew 24:15, referring to Daniel 9:27; 11:31; 12:11), most clearly prefigured in the blasphemous oppression of Israel by Antiochus Epiphanes for three and a half years, a century and a half before Christ was born. A 'man of lawlessness', acknowledging no moral imperative outside his own will, preceded Christ's first advent and will precede his second (2 Thessalonians 2:3).

But it will be the religious rather than the political aspect of this totalitarian regime that is the more serious. Only one religion will be tolerated, headed up by a 'false prophet', second only in importance to the antichrist, empowered by demons to perform deceptive miracles, including 'fire from heaven' and, above all, insisting on the worship of this man who proclaims himself to be God, even setting himself up in God's temple (2 Thessalonians 2:4). The latter text, with Matthew 24, Mark 13 and Luke 21, clearly indicates a seat of government in the Middle East and suggests he may be a Jew (as the late Christian writer, A.W. Pink, asserted in *The Antichrist*, Kregel, 1988) or an Arab, either being able to claim to be a descendant of Abraham. We don't know his name yet, but his number (666) is widely known and its significance will become apparent. It could just mean that in every way he falls short of God's standard, whose perfect number is seven, as is apparent in all the 'sevens' in Revelation (and in the 'week' of divine and human activity, but found nowhere in nature, which is governed by the lunar month and the solar year).

How will the three 'monotheistic' faiths manage, when confronted with this man-made, man-centred, world religion? The choice will be simple: join or be persecuted. Nominal adherents of many faiths will probably accept it, especially if it is a syncretistic amalgam of existing religions, with a new focus of worship and devotion. Again, the story of pre-World War Two Germany springs to mind: political National Socialism became spiritual Naziism, with Adolf Hitler as its prophet in Munich, priest in Nuremberg and king in Berlin, which happened in a 'Christian' country with a Protestant north and a Catholic south.

All who refuse to worship the antichrist or bear his number in order to shop for necessities will risk execution. But God has promised to preserve a limited number of Jews, containing representatives of all twelve tribes of Israel (Revelation 7:2–8). There will be an uncountable number of Christian martyrs coming out of the Big Trouble in a steady stream (Revelation 7:9–17). This will reach a climax in the last city to deserve the name of 'Babylon', a sea port devoted to making money and pursuing pleasure, a 'prostitute' who is 'drunk with the blood of the saints' (Revelation 17:5–6). But those will survive who 'come out of her' and leave urban areas for rural and even the 'wilderness', relying on God to provide for their needs during 1,260 days of terror (Revelation 12:6, the woman here representing the Church in the last days and her unborn child the last converts, even though her 'crown of twelve stars' is now the flag of the European Union).

We are not told what will happen to Muslims. If they persist in regarding Muhammad as the very last prophet and the worship of a human being as the supreme blasphemy, they will suffer with Jews and Christians. If, however, the antichrist and his false prophet arise from the Arab nation, they may well be deceived into thinking this development is both compatible with and even consummatory to their historic faith. It is a case of 'wait and see'.

THE SECOND ADVENT OF THE CHRIST

Christians are astonished when told the Quran accepts the return of Jesus (Isa) to earth, even though there is no mention of Muhammad doing the same. It means Muslims believe he is still alive; actually they believe he never died, much less that he died on a cross, but ascended to heaven while alive.

But there the similarity of faith begins and ends. The simple questions: 'Why is he coming back?' or 'What is he coming back to do?' reveal a yawning gulf between Muslim and Christian expectations, depending on whether the Quran or the Bible is taken to be the true record or revelation of his intentions.

Muslims believe he is returning to demonstrate to the world that he was always a devout Muslim himself and has returned to lead the human race back to the truth of Islam. 'Infidels' who refuse this final opportunity will be killed. Some extremists go further and say he will slaughter all Jews, perhaps forgetting that that would involve his own suicide! After he has accomplished all he has come back to do, he will then die a natural death, for the first time.

Christians believe he is coming back to save Israel 'as a whole', to defeat the antichrist, false prophet and their forces (at the hill of Megiddo or, in Hebrew, *har 'Mageddon*); bind and banish the devil from the earth, later sending him to join his two agents – the antichrist and false prophet – in the fire of hell; reign over the earth with his resurrected followers and particularly his martyred saints, for a long but limited period; call the whole human race, the living and the dead, to his final throne of judgement; and finally to create, with his Father, a new universe in which those who pass the judgement can live for ever.

At least, that's what the book of Revelation says he will do and that's what the early church consistently thought and taught. It was in the fifth century that Augustine changed his mind, halfway through his ministry. It was in reaction to things physical (he called them all 'carnal'), which sprang partly from his youthful promiscuity, partly from his 'neo-platonic' education and partly from over-zealous preaching by others of the physical delights of the Millennium (as Christ's 1,000-year reign had come to be called), not unlike the later Muslim concept of 'Paradise'.

Augustine transferred the reign of Christ with his saints from after his return to before and from earth to heaven. In theological terms; from the pre-millennial to the post-millennial position. This required some juggling with scripture. The last 'seven' in the book of Revelation – after seven letters to seven churches (each with seven parts), and seven seals, seven trumpets and seven bowls – is a series of seven visions (each beginning: 'Then I saw'), bringing history to an end of the old and the beginning of the new. Many miss this final 'seven', because it has been divided between three chapters: Revelation 19, 20 and 21. When the chapter divisions are ignored, it becomes very obvious that the visions present a sequence of final events, each following the previous one ('Then' refers to the events as well as the visions). Augustine's re-arrangement takes number four out of the sequence, leaving the others in their order, and putting it back before number one (that is, 20:1–6 will happen *before* 19:11–21)!

The effect was to switch attention from Christ's coming to reign to his coming to judge and this was incorporated in the Church's creeds. But scripture taken in its plainest, simplest sense clearly says he is coming to do both, first to reign on and over the earth; then, when this planet has disappeared, to judge our race. I have dealt with this controversy about the future in full detail, covering all the different views, in my book: *When Jesus Returns* (Hodder & Stoughton, 1995). I had to mention it briefly here because our understanding of his reign and judgement profoundly affect our views of Islam's future.

If, as I believe, with the early church, he is going to reign on this earth, in bodily form (Bishop Papias, of Hieropolis in Asia, called it his 'corporeal reign on earth'), then a whole lot of biblical statements, both in the Old and New Testaments, about the future of this world, make a whole lot of sense, from Isaiah: 'For the earth will be full of the knowledge of the LORD (i.e. Yahweh) as the waters cover the sea' (11:9) to Revelation: 'the kingdom of the world has become the kingdom of our Lord and of his Christ, and he will reign for ever and ever' (11:15). And both Testaments look forward to the Lord's people sharing in this new worldwide government, from Daniel:

> Then the sovereignty, power and greatness of the kingdoms under the whole heaven will be handed over to the saints, the people of the Most High. His kingdom will be an everlasting kingdom, and all the rulers will worship and obey him (Daniel 7:27)

to Paul: 'Do you not know that the saints will rule the world?' (1 Corinthians 6:2).

This 'Christian' government will bring many benefits to the general populace. Real peace will perhaps be the most welcome. When disputes are settled with full justice, multi-lateral disarmament will follow (Isaiah 2:4). This in turn will lead to prosperity. Better health will mean longer lives (Isaiah 65:20). Even nature will no longer be 'red in tooth and claw', as Tennyson described it (Isaiah 11:6–8, verses immediately following the promise of perfect justice).

But there will be limitations on freedom. Imposed law and order will be welcomed by some but not others. There will be no democracy, no political parties, no debates, no elections, no votes. The king will decide and apply all legislation, as in any true 'kingdom', as opposed to a republic. It will be rule with a rod of iron (Revelation 2:26–7; 12:5), not in the sense of cruel or tyrannous but inflexible and irresistible. Little wonder that the devil, given a final chance, can lead a sizable last-ditch revolt (Revelation 20:7–10).

Above all, there will only be one 'religion'. 'At the name of Jesus every knee should bow, in heaven and on earth and under the earth, and every tongue confess that Jesus Christ is Lord, to the glory of God the Father' (Philippians 2:10–11, quoting Isaiah 45:23 where it is applied to Yahweh, God of Israel).

There will therefore be no place for Islam, or any other religion for that matter. Muslims, who have considered worshipping the man Jesus as divine the greatest blasphemy, will see the error of their ways with their own eyes. The name 'Jesus' will replace 'Allah' on their lips. Their creed will be even shorter than it is now: 'Jesus is Lord', which was the first used by the Church (1 Corinthians 12:3).

I am sadly aware that I have been presenting a minority

view among Christians in Britain, unlike America and many other countries. Most British believers have accepted Augustine's version and are not looking forward to Christ's return to reign on earth. When they daily use the prayer Jesus taught us: 'Your kingdom come . . . on earth as it is in heaven', they are thinking of what the Christ in heaven can enable his church on earth to achieve, either in terms of converting most if not all the population or influencing social and political affairs for the better – all *before* the King of the kingdom gets back. They are therefore unable to endorse my perspective on the replacement of Islam. However, they would simply postpone this until later in the divine programme for the climax of history.

All Christians believe that Jesus, when he returns from heaven, will sooner or later 'judge' the whole human race. Every Christian creed has included a reference: 'from thence he shall come to judge the quick (i.e. the living and moving) and the dead'. Here, we touch on another significant difference between Islam and Christianity, the last one we shall cover in this book.

The Quran teaches and Muslims believe that God will be our judge on the final Day of Judgement. Jesus' claim to be the one before whom the nations will stand, to be separated as sheep from goats (Matthew 25:32), must either be accepted as yet another truthful claim to be divine, or a symptom of schizophrenia or megalomania. As a last desperate resort, the accounts of his teaching must be dismissed as seriously corrupted. Muslims take this last course, though they have no objective reasons for questioning the accuracy of the gospel record, other than its obvious inconsistency with and contradictions to their own scriptures.

Paul makes it quite clear that all human beings will be judged by a human being, one who has faced the moral and social pressures we all face, yet without giving way to them. God has delegated this responsibility to one of us! 'He has set a day when he will judge the world with justice by the *man* he has appointed; he has given proof of this to all men by raising him from the dead' (Acts 17:31), as Paul told the crowds in Athens, later writing to the Christians in Corinth: 'For we must all appear before the judgement seat of Christ, that each one may receive what is due to him for the things done while in the body, whether good or bad' (2 Corinthians 5:10). Some Christians forget all this, assuming that '*him* who was seated on the great white throne' (Rev. 20:11) refers to the Father rather than the Son, but the scriptures we have quoted show that this is not so.

If all human beings who have ever lived are to have their eternal destiny decided by Jesus, that must include all the founders of other religions (like Buddha, Confucius and Muhammad), as well as all the followers. And from the Gospels we have a very good idea what he regards as very serious offences. We take two examples:

Jesus took a very severe view of those who misled others by teaching any other than the truth, the whole truth and nothing but the truth, especially to those who are physically or spiritually immature, unable to discern error. 'It would be better for him to have a large millstone hung around his neck and to be drowned in the sea' (Matthew 18:6); at least that would stop him doing further damage and incurring greater guilt. What must Jesus think about Palestinian children in holiday camps being taught to use lethal weapons, to hate Israelis and Americans, to commit suicidal atrocities and thus make their parents proud of them and their God pleased with them? If this is not wicked, what is?

He also said that the attitude to his followers would be a decisive factor in his verdict. The division between 'sheep and goats' is directly related to what they did, or did not do, to his 'brothers' (Matthew 25:31–46). These have been too narrowly seen as his fellow-Jews or too widely applied to all our fellow-men. The consistent use of the term by Jesus himself and his apostles make it a reference to the disciples of Jesus (John 20:17; Hebrews 2:11). To serve them is to serve him. To make them suffer is to make him suffer, as Paul discovered on the Damascus road (Acts 9:5). Muslims need to realise this too. The majority of Christians suffering and dying for their faith today do so under Islamic government, from Indonesia through Pakistan and Arabia to Sudan and Nigeria. May the followers of Islam find salvation before it is too late, and find it through the very person they are tormenting, the one who prayed as he died on a cross: 'Father, forgive them, for they do not know what they are doing' (Luke 23:34), which later drew the response from one of his executioners: 'Surely he was the Son of God' (Matthew 27:54). And one of the first to benefit from Jesus dying in his place, quite literally, was a terrorist called 'Barabbas' (it is ironic that his surname means 'Son of Father' and even more that one early manuscript records his forename as 'Jesus', meaning 'Saviour', in quite common use at that time).

To conclude, the ultimate hope of Christ's return to earth throws a very different light on the current Islamic resurgence. Though in the immediate future it presents the greatest challenge (some would say 'threat', but I have chosen not to) to Christians, all who believe the Bible to be God's word of truth can come to only one conclusion: the days of Islam are numbered.

Epilogue

THE STRESS WITHIN THE BOOK

The core of the burden in my heart and the book in your hand is in the second half, not the first, and more particularly in Chapters 8, 9 and 10. I dare to claim more 'inspired' value in these than any of the others.

As already mentioned, the three titles came to me in a flash, when I asked the Lord what aspects of the present state of his Church in Britain he was most concerned about. As I further meditated on them in succeeding months, the contents also poured into my mind.

It was therefore a great disappointment when some listeners and viewers of the recorded version expressed more interest in the first half of the message ('The Islamic Resurgence') than the second ('The Christian Response'). Of course, that was new to them and the novel always appeals. And it contained the most sensational statement, which the media, true to form, was quick to latch on to.

But apart from this prediction about the future role of Islam in Britain and the identification of its real source, most of the first section was simply information gathered, rather laboriously, from sources available to anyone else, from press cuttings to larger publications, many of which are written by authors with far more experience than I, some Muslim and some Christian. I am what the French call a 'vulgariser', someone who takes scholarly findings and makes them available and edible to the 'common' people. I am content with that role, not unlike that of my Lord Jesus himself, of whom it was said that 'the common people heard him gladly', a tribute to them as well as him. They know when they are listening to someone who knows what he's talking about.

My message is not so much about Islam as about Christianity. It is not addressed to Muslims, though I hope if some read it they will get a real understanding of the Christian gospel. But it is addressed to Christians, who need to study their own faith even more than that of others, as well as the way in which they live it out. That is one reason why I have included Bible references but not chapter and verse numbers for the Quran.

Perhaps the titles of the three crucial chapters will tempt some Christians to give them less careful attention or even skip over them altogether. The words are so common in Christian discourse, well-worn and even out-worn, that familiarity has bred contempt. But I used them because I believe they were God-given. Sometimes we need repetition to avoid the danger of taking things for granted. One listener to the original message said of these three parts: 'David, I've heard you say all this before', and his tone was one of mild rebuke. Later I thought of what I should have replied (repartee usually crops up too late!): 'Yes, and I'll say it again, and again, and again, until Christians wake up and realise how important these three things are to God and how vital to the Church.'

One encouraging type of comment has converged on the

Trinitarian focus of all three chapters. Some have realised more than ever before how fundamental to our faith and life is the revelation of God as three persons in one. Others have seen for the first time that this is the major difference between Christianity and all other religions, especially Islam. Still others have generously commented that at last they have begun to understand the meaning and significance of 'the Trinity', not as a dogma but as the dynamic of salvation. They have 'got the message'.

The only true/real God who exists is Father, Son and Holy Spirit. The only real relationship with him is a personal, intimate knowledge of all three. And only the work of all three can produce a righteousness acceptable to God and fit for his new world.

These are the fundamental features of genuine Christianity and the three chapters could almost be taken out of the book and stand on their own as a manual of the gospel. But they are here because they are directly relevant to a confrontation with resurgent Islam.

Many Christians in Britain are already living in situations dominated by this unfamiliar religion, though this is more true of urban than suburban districts. They are already experiencing the pressures this brings and the dilemmas it raises. Since more and more of us are going to find ourselves in the same circumstances, some questions spontaneously spring to mind, to which Chapters 8, 9 and 10 of this book provide clues to the answers.

WILL WE SURVIVE?

The historical record is not encouraging. Whenever Islam has spread in strength, the Christian Church has tended to disappear. There were Christian communities in Arabia at the time of Muhammad. There are none at all now, though there may be some 'secret believers' and a few discreet groups of expatriate workers in the oil and building industries. The coast of North Africa was once a Christian stronghold. For centuries it became a blank on the Christian map, with the exception of the Coptic remnant in Egypt, and only recently have a few missions been able to penetrate some parts again. Will this happen in Britain?

It could, but it need not. A Church strong in the three dimensions of reality, relationship and righteousness will survive, particularly with the third. Did not God promise Habakkuk that 'the righteous will survive by keeping faith' (see Habakkuk 2:4)? But the general level in the British Church today is not up to it. Unless there is a radical change (which is what repentance is), much of the Church could disappear, but I believe a remnant will remain and, having been refined by the removal of the nominal, would be in a much better state to be used by God to do his will and work.

But is the question itself a valid one for Christians to ask or even consider? Jesus told his disciples that a concern for self-preservation was the route to extinction (Matthew 16:25). If this is true for individual followers, how much more for their communities. Paradoxically, we are more likely to survive if we are not concerned whether we do or not!

WILL WE SUFFER?

The geographical record is not encouraging. There are more Christian martyrs today than ever before. Where are Christians facing most persecution for their faith? Eastern Indonesia, Southern Sudan and Central Nigeria immediately spring to mind, all areas controlled by a Muslim majority. As we have already said, the attitude of Muslims towards Christians can only be truly gauged when they have gained political, military and social power, not when they are a religious minority primarily concerned with their own rights, identity and survival.

Now the three dimensions have the opposite effect. The stronger they are, the more likely is both our survival and our suffering! The more sure we are that our God is the only real one, the greater is the challenge to those who believe other-wise. Maybe some day a Muslim will write a book entitled: *The Challenge of Christianity to Muslims*! I wish I could have done that but felt quite unable to do so. Suffice it to say that ascendant Islam does not easily tolerate rival faiths. Tension builds and sooner or later violence erupts.

Again, is this a valid question? Jesus' honesty shows in his predictions of suffering for his followers, wherever they lived or whatever faiths they encountered. He called them to 'follow' in his footsteps, which led straight to the cross. He promised that in the world they would have trouble, big trouble. He predicted they would be hated as he was hated. The way to glory is through suffering; it was for him and will be for us.

In other words, suffering is the normal state of the Christian and will be particularly aggravated by our righteousness. Centuries before Jesus, a Greek philosopher said that if ever there was a perfect man in the world, he would be assassinated. 'In fact, everyone who wants to live a godly life in Christ Jesus will be persecuted' (2 Timothy 3:12). That is our calling. That is what we can expect, whether under Islam or not.

WILL WE SWELL?

The two previous questions considered are of the flesh, not the spirit. They express natural anxieties, but are focused on ourselves rather than others. Even this third question can spring from the same motivation, depending on why it is asked. Will we get many converts? Will we persuade many Muslims to leave their faith and come over to ours? Will the Church grow and become bigger again? A declining Church can become obsessed with 'church growth' principles, seizing on any method that might swell numbers. Even evangelism can be inspired by a desire to fill empty pews.

But this third question can be asked, and needs to be in a very different way. Will we be so much more concerned about the salvation of others than our own success that we shall be used by God to set many free from their sins, their power in this life and penalty in the next? Will the surviving, suffering Church be a channel of grace to the lost? Will our prime concern be the spreading of the gospel, even when 'proselytising' becomes illegal? Will Muslims bless the day when they heard it from us? Will we do all we can to introduce them to the freedom of the sons of God, regardless of cost or consequence?

The short answer is that if we can't do it now, we won't do it then. Doing it either now *and* then, however, depends on the vital three dimensions again and particularly the relationship we enjoy and the righteousness we exhibit, which are the living proof we have found reality and an encouragement to others to seek the same. Wasn't it the philosopher Nietzsche, the man behind Hitler, who said: 'I'd want to be saved if Christians looked more saved'? Muslims must not be allowed to make the same observation if we are to earn the right to share our faith with them.

*   *   *

This, then, is why I have written this epilogue: to stress the importance of Chapters 8, 9 and 10. I believe they contain the merciful guidance of our heavenly Father on how to be prepared for the future, whatever it holds. It has always been his practice to tell his people what is going to happen to them and how to be ready for it. He is never surprised or caught unawares. So we need never be, either.

I am going to suggest something I have never done before in any of my books. If you have persevered and stayed with me right to the end, I want you now to go back and read again those vital three chapters, even on your knees, asking the Lord to show if you are fully ready and, if not, how you can be. I know the Lord will bless you as you do so. I thank him for this opportunity to share my heart, and I believe his too.

Appendix

HABAKKUK 3

In Chapter 7 I have explained how this 'minor' prophet's ministry and message came to be associated with this book of mine about Islam and Christians, and how his mood was changed from dread to delight as he contemplated future events affecting his people. His final 'sermon' was actually a song and he commissioned a composer to arrange it and an orchestra to accompany it.

Years ago I transposed its contents into modern verse but could neither write a tune for it nor find one of the right metre in any hymn book. On a visit to South Africa, in the days of apartheid, I learned that it would fit the tune of their national anthem, but for political reasons I could not use it. Moving on to Zimbabwe, I was told that the former national anthem of Rhodesia had been set to the same tune and it could now be used. It was Beethoven's 'Ode to joy' (how appropriate!) from his Ninth Symphony.

So I came back to England with words and music. Imagine my surprise to hear that a fellowship in the north of England had been told (through a word of prophecy) to learn this very tune but to wait for the words to be given to them. They were getting tired of humming the melody without the lyrics and even made one abortive attempt to write them. Imagine their excitement when their pastor returned with the words from a Bournemouth conference where I had read my version. Here they are:

Lord, your fame has gone before you,
From the time your arm was bared;
Tales of deeds so overwhelming,
Even listening makes me scared!
Now, today, O Lord, repeat them,
Prove that you are still the same –
But in wrath remember mercy
For the honour of your name.

Look! this holy God descending
Spreads the sky with glorious rays.
Trailing from his hand of power –
Earth is filled with sound of praise.
But the guilty nations tremble,
Plague and pestilence their fears;
Even ancient mountains crumble
When the infinite appears.

Are you angry with the rivers?
Is your wrath upon the streams?
Do you rage against the ocean
With your horse and chariot teams?
Writhing hills and flooded valleys,
Sun and moon stand still with fear
At the glint of flying arrows,
Lightning of your flashing spear.

Striding through the earth in vengeance,
Threshing nations till it's done –
All to save your chosen people,
Rescue your anointed one!
You have crushed the wicked leader,
Stripped him bare and split his head:
So his storming, gloating warriors
Scatter to the wind instead.

Having heard the final outcome,
Knowing all and not just part,
Great emotions grip my body,
Quivering lips and pounding heart.
Trembling legs give way beneath me –
Yet with patience will I wait.
When the foe invades my country,
Certain of his dreadful fate.

Though the fig tree does not blossom
And the vine is void of grapes,
Though the olive trees are barren
And the fields produce no crops,
Though no lambs are in the sheep-fold
And no cattle in the stall –
Yet will I enjoy my Saviour
Glad that God is all in all.

Joyfully I face the future
With my failing strength restored
And my angry questions answered
By this marvellous sovereign Lord.
See my heart and feet are leaping
Like a deer upon the heights!
Set my words to holy music,
Voices and stringed instruments.

The reader is also recommended to listen to the series of tapes expounding the book of Habakkuk, which are available from:

Anchor Recordings
72 The Street
Kennington
Ashford
Kent
TN24 9HS
England

Phone and Fax: 01233 620958